Melita Illyrica and *Melita Africana*: The Islands of Saint Paul

Noel Muscat ofm
Sandro Tomašević ofm

Foreword by Chev. Prof. Horatio C.R. Vella

Malta 2018

Published in collaboration with
The Holy Land Commissariat, Malta

Front cover picture:
Ancient map of the Mediterranean showing the various names of the internal seas,and the islands of Melita in the Adriatic (Mljet) and Melita in the Mare Libicum (Malta)

ISBN 978-99957-1-395-9

Printed in Malta
Best Print Co Ltd.

Dedicated to our beloved late mothers
Lina and Zlata

Contents

Foreword

I have known Fr Noel Muscat O.F.M. from a pilgrimage to the Holy Land he conducted some years ago which my son and I participated in. From the thorough information and explanations he gave us on the holy places and the political history of Israel, I can say that this is the same person who here appears as a balanced commentator on an issue which also here bears the element of the divide. I have also known Fr Muscat as the Guardian of the Monastery of the Holy Sepulchre in Jerusalem, appearing then as a strict superior but benevolent at the same time: these two qualities re-appear in this present commentary, strictness to his sources and kindness in his judgement regarding the opinions on Mljet. Finally, I have known Fr Muscat at the Monastery of St Mary of Jesus in Valletta, introducing me to the work I am presently carrying out at that same monastery at its Provincial Archives: here he appears as both knowledgeable and humble: qualities one can also see in this work.

Indeed, here Fr Noel makes several humble statements. He thinks highly of scholars, not so of his own work. Anybody familiar with the Maltese version of the *Terra Sancta* is used to his writings which go into details and which are so enriching with important information on the history of the Franciscans in the Holy Land. Maybe he thinks that one must be an expert in one thing: this is not humility, but good sense. But then a scholar should not be narrowed down by what he is an expert in: on the contrary, his horizons are widened to so many other spheres. This reminds us of what Cicero says in the *Pro Archia*, that all subjects are somehow interwoven one with another. Fr Noel is an expert in Franciscan history and spirituality: it is for this reason that he qualifies to be a writer on related subjects, such as that of St Paul's shipwreck.

What motivated primarily Fr Noel in writing this commentary is the opportunity he had of being in two places which refer to the same event. He first visited these locations, then he was inspired to write about them, and finally he researched on them. Very often, scholars do not have such an opportunity of visiting places they write about. Herodotus and Pausanias made it a point to do so in Classical times. Some modern scholars write on subjects they are far from familiar with. On the contrary, as a Franciscan Friar and Catholic priest from Malta, and having been twice on the island of Mljet, such a contribution must bear appropriate motivation.

Fr Muscat does not hide his feelings: he claims he is biased toward one of the two islands which claimed to have received St Paul on his journey to Rome. But this bias is not only personal, having been born on Malta and having heard so much on "our" St Paul in "in our island"; but it is also scholarly and properly weighed as a scholar ought to weigh arguments. His conclusion is one: that not enough archaeological evidence can give the final stamp to what appears to be the more persuading in argument. He, despite the fact that he is priest, does not accept at face value certain traditions, particularly that the Gozitans heard the preaching of St Paul in Naxxar. He throws doubts on whether Publius, Roman Governor of Malta, could have been ordained Bishop. Certainly, and this is to be noted, he never calls him "St Publius".

Fr Muscat knows me as a familiar name in such matters as Maltese history. It is for this reason that I have been consulted for the revision of his work. He knows that when I was a student at the University of Malta, I was then asked to translate Jean Quintin's *Insulae Melitae descriptio*, published in 1536, to make a new edition of the work and to write a commentary on it, which edition with translation and commentary was published in 1980 through my *The earliest description of Malta in Latin (Lyons, 1536)*. Thanks to Latin, I was introduced to Melitensia Studies, and forty years ago I read in Latin the two works analyzed and consulted by Fr Muscat for this work, those of Georgius and Ciantar.

I too have gone into the question of the site of St Paul's shipwreck in Malta because Jean Quintin had gone into this issue before us. And I consider that Jean Quintin is the most important and among the most ancient sources for the exact site of the shipwreck, even if Fr Noel repeatedly says that this cannot be proved and has not been proved for lack of archaeological evidence derived from the bottom of the sea. The problem here is that although several anchors from Roman times have been found, none will bear the name of St Paul or the name of the boat which brought him here. But Jean Quintin is the most important because, as he himself said, he did *not* believe that St Paul came here, but to Mljet. It is for this very reason that it is the most important source, because it is an unbiased report based upon the information he received from the Maltese residents at the time of the coming of the Knights of St John to Malta in 1530, whom he described as experts in navigation.

In his account, Jean Quintin reports on a very long tradition which the Maltese residents then had kept from immemorial times. His words *Ibi vetustissime*, referring to the jut of land separating the beach within a bay at St Paul's Bay, and to the site of the church built close by the site of the shipwreck, confirm that the site and name of the locality were not invented by the Order of St John, but existed long before and kept alive by tradition which counts for unwritten history.

Fr Muscat also knew I translated a long poem from Greek into English written on Gozo in the 12th century A.D. by a Byzantine exile. The remarkable thing about this poet is, that despite the fact that he was Greek and belonging to the Orthodox Rite, he felt no antagonism or repugnance at calling "the other island", that is, Malta, as the island of the shipwreck of St Paul. As Greek Orthodox, one expected him to opt for Mljet instead, an island which in ancient times belonged to the Greek world.

The importance of Fr Noel Muscat's work is to be seen as a review of a controversy which in the past was passionate, but today it is cool and free from prejudice. Its importance is increased by the fact that the author of this work has been on both sites which claim St Paul's shipwreck. Furthermore, the author is highly cognizant of the relationships between the Orthodox and the Latin Rites which in the past pulled the story of the shipwreck to their own interests: indeed, Fr Noel served for many years, as he still does, as a Franciscan in the Holy Land where, especially at the Shrine of the Holy Sepulchre where he was Guardian at the Franciscan monastery, and where the two religions often got entangled in their passionate care for the sacred vestiges.

May this work help in encouraging historians and archaeologists in both Mljet and Malta further their studies on such an important event in our common history.

Chev. Prof. Horatio Caesar Roger Vella
4th June, 2018

Select Bibliography

Sources

ABELA G.F. (1647), *Della Descrittione di Malta, isola nel Mare Siciliano, con le sue antichità ed altre notizie, divisa in quattro libri*, Malta.

AGIUS DE SOLDANIS G.P.F. (1757), *Discours apologétique contre la dissertation historique et critique sur le naufrage de St. Paul dans la Mer Adriatique, pubbliée par Mr. l'Abbé Ladvocat, bibliothecaire de la Sorbonne*, Avignon.

AGIUS DE SOLDANIS G.P.F. (1758), *Discorso Apologetico intorno al Naufragio di S. Paolo Apostolo*, Venezia.

APOLLONIUS OF RHODES (2015), *Agronautica*, Book IV (Cambridge Greek and Latin Classics), edited by R. Hunter, Cambridge University Press.

AQUILINA G. – FIORINI S. (ed.) (2001), *Documentary Sources of Maltese History. Part IV. Documents at the Vatican. No. 1 Archivio Segreto Vaticano. Congregazione Vescovi e Regolari. Malta: Visita Apostolica no. 51 Mgr Petrus Dusina, 1575*, University of Malta.

BRES O. (1872), *Malta Antica Illustrata*, Roma.

BUSUTTIL J. – FIORINI S. – VELLA H.C.R. (2010), *Tristitia ex Melitogaudo. Lament in Greek Verse of a XIIth-century Exile on Gozo*, Malta.

CHRYSOSTOMUS IOANNES, *In Acta Apostolorium,* Hom. LIV, in MIGNE J.P., *Patrologia Cursus Completus. Series Graeca*, Vol. 60, col. 373-374.

CIANTAR G.A. (1738), *De B. Paulo Apostolo in Melitam Siculo Adriatici Maris Insulam Naufragio ejecto dissertationes apologeticae*. In inspectiones anticriticas R.P.D. Ignatii Georgii de Melitensi Apostoli Naufragio, descripto in Act. Apost. Cap. XXVII & XXVIII, Venice.

CIANTAR G.A. (1763), *Critica dei critici moderni, che dall'anno 1730 infino al 1760 scrissero sulla controversia del naufragio di s. Paolo apostolo, descritto nei Capi 27 e 28 degli Atti apostolici*, Venice.

CIANTAR G.A. (1772-1780), *Malta illustrata ovvero descrizione di Malta isola del Mare Siciliano e Adriatico, con le sue antichità ed altre notizie, divisa in quattro libri, del commendatore fra Giovanfrancesco Abela, vicecancelliere della Sagra ed Eminentissima Religione Gerosolimitana, corretta, accresciuta e continovata dal conte Giovannantonio Ciantar*, 2 volumes *in folio*, Malta.

CONSTANTINE PORPHYROGENITUS (1985^2), *De Administrando Imperio*, 36, Greek text edited by G.Y. MORAVCSIK, English translation by R.J.H. JENKINS, New revised edition, Washington D.C.

ĐURĐEVIĆ I., (1726), *L'onore della venuta di S. Paolo Apostolo restituito a Melita Illiricana ovvero La confutazione degli Apologisti Maltese, contendenti esser in Malta sorto l'Apostolo Paolo dopo il famoso naufragio riferito da S. Luca in capitolo XXVII e XXVIII degli Apostolici Atti. Discorso di Dn. Ignazio Giorgi, Abate di Meleda composto a istanza del Sig.r Arcidiacono Capor Vicario generale in Curzola 1726*. Manuscript 106. Archives of the Franciscan Friary, Dubrovnik.

ĐURĐEVIĆ I. (1730), *Divus Paulus Apostolus in mari, quod nunc Ventus sinus dicitur, naufragus et Melitae Dalmatensis insulae post naufragium hospes sive de genuino significatu duorum locorum in Actibus Apostolicis*. Cap. XXVII,27. Navigantibus nobis in Adria. Cap. XXVIII,1. Tunc cognovimus quia Melita insula vocabatur. Inspectiones anticriticae auctore D. Ignatio Georgio, Benedictino e congregatione Melitensi Ragusina. Adjicitur brevis Dissertatio eiudem Auctoris de Catellis Melitaeis, Venice.

JEAN QUINTIN D'AUTUN (1536), *Insulæ Melitæ descriptio ex commentariis rerum quotidianarum*, Lyons.

Studies

ACWORTH A. (1973), *Where was St. Paul Shipwrecked? A Re-examination of the Evidence*, in *Journal of Theological Studies* 24, 190-193.

AQUILINA Ġ. (2011), *Il-Franġiskani Maltin (Ta' Ġieżu) 1482c - 1965c,* Klabb Kotba Maltin, Malta.

AZZOPARDI J. (ed.) (1990), *St. Paul's Grotto, Church and Museum at Rabat, Malta*, Malta.

AZZOPARDI J. (ed.) (2006), *The Cult of St Paul in the Christian Churches and in the Maltese Tradition. Il culto di San Paolo nelle chiese cristiane e nella tradizione maltese*, (Wignacourt Museum, Rabat – Malta, XXV Anniversary Celebrations. Acts of the International Symposium, 26-27 June 2006) Malta.

AZZOPARDI J. (2006), *Juan Benegas de Cordoba: l'eremita che trasferì la Grotta di San Paolo all'Ordine Gerosolimitano*, in J. AZZOPARDI (ed.), *The Cult of St Paul in the Christian Churches and in the Maltese Tradition*, (Acts of the International Symposium, 26-27 June 2006) Malta, 173-190.

AZZOPARDI J. - PACE A. (ed.) (2010), *San Pawl f'Malta u l-formazzjoni ta' identità ta' nazzjon. St Paul in Malta and the shaping of a nation's identity*, Office of the Prime Minister, Valletta – Malta.

BONANNO A. (2005), *Malta. Phoenician, Punic and Roman*, Midsea Books, Malta.

BORG M. (2014), *The Cave Churches in Malta and their Paintings. An Art Historical Gazetteer*, University of Malta Library, Electronic Theses & Dissertations (ETD) Repository, Malta.

BUHAGIAR K. (1997), *The San Niklaw Cave-Settlement*, in *Melita Historica* 12/2, 131-138.

BUHAGIAR M. (1983), *The Study of the Maltese Paleochristian Catacombs*, in *Melita Historica* 8/4, 291-298.

BUHAGIAR M. (1990), *The St. Paul's Cave Complex at Rabat, Malta, and its Archaeological Significance*, in J. AZZOPARDI (ed.), *St. Paul's Grotto, Church and Museum at Rabat, Malta*, Progress Press, Malta, 51-64.

BUHAGIAR M. (1993), *The St. Paul Shipwreck Controversy: An assessment of the source material*, in *Proceedings of History* Week, Malta Historical Society, 181-213.

BUHAGIAR M. (1996), *The Early Christian Remains at Tas-Silġ and San Pawl Milqi, Malta. A Reconsideration of the Archaeological Evidence*, in *Melita Historica* 12, 1-41.

BUHAGIAR M. (1998), *The Iconography of the Maltese rock-cut Tombs, Punico-Hellenistic, Paleochristian and Byzantine*, in *Melita Historica* 12/3, 221-238.

BUHAGIAR M. (2002), *The Re-Christianization of Malta; Siculo-Greek Monasticism, Dejr Toponyms, and Rock-cut Churches*, in *Melita Historica* 13/3, 253-283.

BUHAGIAR M. (2006), *St. Paul Shipwreck and Early Christianity in Malta*, in *The Cult of St. Paul in the Christian Churches and in the Maltese Tradition*, ed. J. AZZOPARDI (Acts of the International Symposium, 26-27 June) Malta, 155-160.

BUSCEMI A.M. (1997[2]), *San Paolo. Vita, Opera, Messaggio*, Franciscan Printing Press (Studium Biblicum Franciscanum, Analecta, 43), Jerusalem.

BUZOV M. (2012), *Is Mljet – Melita in Dalmatia the Island of St. Paul's Shipwreck?*, in *Historia Antiqua*, 21, Zagreb, 491-505.

BUZOV M. (2013), *Mjlet / Melita in Dalmatia is the Island of St. Paul's Shipwreck (The Ragusan Tradition on St. Paul's Shipwreck)*, in *Classica et Christiana*, 8/2, Institute of Archeology, Zagreb, 395-422.

CASSAR PULLICINO J. (1944), *Pauline Traditions in Malta*, in *Scientia* 10, 19-31.

DEMOVIĆ M. (2008), *A Study accompanying Croatian translation of the Đurđević's Book on Saint Paul's Shipwreck on the Island of Mljet*, in ĐURĐEVIĆ I., *Sveti Pavao apostol brodlomac (St. Paul the Apostle Castaway)*, Dubrovnik, 2008.

DEMOVIĆ M. (2015), *Three famous Shipwreck Survivors from Dubrovnik,* in PAVETIĆ Z. (ed.), *The Journey of Paul the Apostle to Rome led over the Croatian Island of Mljet (Melita) / Put apostola Pavla za Rim vodio je preko hrvatskog otoka Mljeta (Melite)*, Proceedings of the academic conference held on Mljet, 15 October 2011, Zagreb 2015.

FARRUGIA RANDON S., *Comino, Filfla and St. Paul's Island*, Malta 1995.

FERRES A. (1866), *Descrizione Storica delle Chiese di Malta e Gozo*, Malta 1866.

FIORINI S. – VELLA H.C.R. (2006), *New XIIIth Century Evidence for the Pauline Tradition and Christianity in the Maltese Islands*, in *The Cult of St. Paul in the Christian Churches and in the Maltese Tradition*, AZZOPARDI J. (ed.) (Acts of the International Symposium 26-27 June) Malta, 161-172.

FIORINI S. (2010), *The Cult of St Paul in Medieval Malta*, in AZZOPARDI J. – PACE A. (ed.), *San Pawl f'Malta u l-formazzjoni ta' identità ta' nazzjon. St Paul in Malta and the shaping of a nation's identity*, Office of the Prime Minister, Valletta – Malta, 83-97.

FRELLER TH. (2006), *St Paul's Grotto, Malta, and its Antidotic earth in the awareness of early Modern Europe*, in AZZOPARDI J. (ed.), *The Cult of St Paul in the Christian Churches and in the Maltese Tradition*, (Acts of the International Symposium, 26-27 June) Malta, 191-218.

GALEA J. (1960), *Bibliography of the Shipwreck of St. Paul*, in *Scientia* 26, 84-96.

GALEA J. (1990), *Grand Master Aloph de Wignacourt annexes to St. Paul's Grotto the Church of the Shipwreck at St. Paul's Bay*, in AZZOPARDI J. (ed.), *St. Paul's Grotto, Church and Museum at Rabat,* Malta, 69-74.

GAMBIN B. ET ALII (2016), *7300 Years of Vegetation History and Climate for NW Malta: a Holocene perspective*, Institut Méditerranéen de Biodiversité et d'Ecologie marine et continentale (IMBE), Aix Marseille Université, CNRS, IRD, Avignon Université, Bâtiment Villemin, BP 80, 13545 Aix-en-Provence CEDEX 04, France 2016; Institute of Earth Systems, University of Malta, Msida, Malta, https://www.clim-past.net/12/273/2016/cp-12-273-2016.pdf (accessed 5 December 2017).

GILL J., *Commentary on Acts 27:35*, in *The New John Gill Exposition of the Entire Bible*, (http://www.studylight.org/commentaries/gebh/acts-27.html.) (accessed 8 September 2017).

GLIUBICH S., *Giorgi Ignazio*, in *Dizionario Biografico degli Uomini Illustri della Dalmazia*, Vienna-Zara, 1856, 145-150.

GORDINI G.D. (1968), *Publio, vescovo di Atene*, in *Bibliotheca Sanctorum*, Città Nuova Editrice, Roma, Vol. 10, 1237.

GOZZO S. (1963), *L'apostolo Paolo da Malta a Reggio – Atti 28,11-13a*, in MARIANI B. (ed)., *San Paolo. Da Cesarea a Roma. Esegesi, Storia, Topografia, Archeologia*, Torino, 43-46.

JELIĆ D. - BUDINSKI I. - LAUŠ B. (2012), *Distribution and conservation status of the batrarcho and herpetofauana of the Croatian island of Mljet*, in *Herpetozoa* 24 (3/4), Vienna, 165-178.

JOHNSON L.T. (1992), *Sacra Pagina. The Acts of the Apostles* (*Sacra Pagina Series*, Vol. 5), Minnesota.

HEMER C.J. (1975), *Euroaquilo and Melita*, in *Journal of Theological Studies* 26,100-111.

HIRSCHFELD N. (1990), *The Ship of Saint Paul. Historical Background*, in *Biblical Archeologist* 53, 25-39.

LATTEY G. (1949), *The Harbour Phoenix*, in *Scripture* 4, 144-146.

MAISTRELLO I. (1963), *Il Viaggio di S. Paolo da Cesarea a Roma alla luce della scienza nautica. Atti 27,1-28,14*, in MARIANI B. (ed)., *San Paolo. Da Cesarea a Roma. Esegesi, Storia, Topografia, Archeologia*, Torino, 163-192.

Malta Herpetological Society, *Maltese Herpetofauna*, in http://mhs.org.mt/Knowledgebase/localfauna (accessed 5 December 2017);

Mangion G. (1981), *Ciantar Giovanni Antonio,* in *Dizionario Biografico degli Italiani (Treccani),* Vol. 25, Roma.

Mariani B. (ed). (1963), *San Paolo. Da Cesarea a Roma. Esegesi, Storia, Topografia, Archeologia*, Torino.

Meinardus O.F.A. (1974), *Melita Illyrica or Africana. An Examination of the Site of St. Paul's Shipwreck*, in *Ostkirchliche Studien* 23, 21-36.

Meinardus O.F.A. (1976), *St. Paul Shipwrecked in Dalmatia*, in *Biblical Archaeologist* 39, 145-147.

Messina A. (1989), *Troglodismo Medievale a Malta*, in *Melita Historica* 10/2, 109-120.

Mifsud S. (2014), *Which Viper bit Saint Paul in Malta*, in *The Times of Malta* (19 February), https://www.timesofmalta.com/articles/view/20140219/opinion/Which-viper-bit-St-Paul-in-Malta-.507396 (accessed 5 December 2017).

Ničetić A. (2000), *O nekim navigačijskim aspektima plovidve Svetog Pavla od Krete do Melite,* in *Anali Dubrovnik* 38, Dubrovnik, 305-307.

Olgivie R.M. (1958), *Phoenix*, in *Journal of Theological Studies* 9, 308-314.

Palunko V. (1910), *Melita del naufragio di S. Paolo e isola Meleda in Dalmazia*, Spalato.

Palunko V. (2009), *Melita otok brodoloma Sv. Pavla jest otok Mljet u Dalmacji*, Zagreb.

Pavetić Z. (ed.) (2015), *The Journey of Paul the Apostle to Rome led over the Croatian Island of Mljet (Melita). Put Apostola Pavla za rim vodio je preko Hrvatskog Otoka Mljeta (Melite)*. Proceedings of the Academic Conference held on Mljet (Melita) (15 October 2011). Zbornik Radova Znanstyenog Skupa Održanog na Mljetu (Meliti) (15 listopada 2011), Zagreb.

Rešetar M. (1926), *Djela Ignacija Gorgi (Ignata Đorđiča)*, Na svijet izdala Jugoslavenska Akademija Znanosti i Umjetnosti, u Zagrebu.

Saydon P.P. (1962), *The Site of Saint Paul's Shipwreck*, in *Melita Theologica* 14/1-2, 58-61.

Schaff Ph. (2002), *Saint Chrysostom: Homilies on the Acts of the Apostles and the Epistle to the Romans*, Christian Classics Etherial Library, Grand Rapids, Michigan.

Schembri G. (1963), *Il naufragio di S. Paolo a Malta*, in Mariani B. (ed)., *San Paolo. Da Cesarea a Roma. Esegesi, Storia, Topografia, Archeologia*, Torino, 31-40.

Smith J. (1880), *The Voyage and Shipwreck of St. Paul. With Dissertations on the Life and Writings of St. Luke, and the Ships and Navigation of the Antients*, 4th edition, Longmans, Green and Co., London.

Springer Z., *Island of Mljet. Is Island of Mljet Homer's Ogygia?*, www.croatianhistory.net (accessed 18 June 2017).

Stošić J. (1998), *Benediktinski samostan Sv. Marije na Mljetu*, Radovi Instituta za povijest umjetnosti 22, 7-21.

TAMMUZ O. (2005), *Mare clausum? Sailing Seasons in the Mediterranean in Early Antiquity*, in *Mediterranean Historical Review,* Vol. 20, No. 2, 145-162.

TRUMP D.H. (1972), *Malta. An Archaeological Guide,* London.

TRUMP D.H. (2002), *Malta Prehistory and Temples*, Midsea Books Ltd. Malta.

TURKOVIĆ T. (2011), *The Late Antique "Palace" in Polače Bay (Mljet) – Tetrachic "Palace"?*, Paper submitted at the Faculty of Humanities and Social Sciences, Department of History, (Hortus Artium Medievalium, Brepols Publishers, Vol. 17, 211-233), University of Zagreb.

VELLA H.C.R. (1980), *Quintinus (1536) and the St. Paul's Shipwreck in Malta*, in *Melita Historica* 8/1, 61-64.

VELLA H.C.R. (1980), *The Earliest Description of Malta (Lyons 1536) by Jean Quintin d'Autun*, Translation and Notes, Malta.

VELLA H.C.R. (1982), *Quintinus (1536) and the Temples of Juno and Hercules in Malta*, in *Athenaeum*, Vol. 60 (1,2), 272-276.

VELLA H.C.R. (1995), *The Island of Gozo in Classical Texts. Occasional Papers on Islands and Small States*. Valletta, Malta, Foundation for International Studies: Islands and Small States Institute, University of Malta.

VELLA H.C.R. (2002), *Malta u Għawdex fl-era klassika*, in *Kullana Kulturali* 38, Malta.

VELLA H.C.R. (2012), *The Origin of the Name of Gozo*, in *The Gozo Observer* 27, 2-20.

VELLA H.C.R. (2012), *Thrinacia, the Island of Malta*, in *Literatura*. Research Journal for Literary Scholarship, 54 (3) 7-36, Vilnius.

WATTS-PLUMPKIN E. (2013), *Tas-Silġ, Malta. From prehistoric temple to Byzantine church*, in *World Archaeology* 59, https://www.world.archaeology.com (accessed 8 September 2017).

WHITE J. (2001), *Evidence and Paul's Journeys. An Historical Investigation into the Travels of the Apostle Paul*, Hilliard, Ohio.

WYATT H.V. (2005), *How Themistocles Zammit found Malta Fever (brucellosis) to be transmitted by the milk of goats*, in *Journal of the Royal Society of Medicine*, Volume 98 (10), 451-454.

ZAMMIT W.L. (2006), *Grand Master Aloph de Wignacourt's foundation for St Paul's Grotto, 1619*, in AZZOPARDI J. (ed.), *The Cult of St Paul in the Christian Churches and in the Maltese Tradition*, (Acts of the International Symposium, 26-27 June) Malta, 219-235.

List of Plates

21. ENE (Grigal) Gale at entrance to Grand Harbour, Malta
22. San Pawl Milqi chapel, Malta
23. St. Paul's Grotto, Rabat
24. Għajn Rażul, St. Paul's Bay, Malta
25. Fanum Iunonis. Archaeological remains at Tas-Silġ
26. View of St. Paul's Bay, with Selmunett Islet on the left and Qawra point on the right
27. Pietro Paolo Novelli, St. Paul healing Publius' father. Chapel of St. Trophimus, Ta' Ġieżu Church, Valletta (1632)
28. Guido Reni (1575-1642), Saint Paul the Apostle

Introduction

Paul of Tarsus was on his way to Rome from Caesarea in Palestine, held as a prisoner who had been unjustly accused in front of the Roman governor by the Jewish establishment of defiling the Temple of Jerusalem by introducing pagans in it, with the result that he had to appeal his case before the emperor. It was the autumn of A.D. 60 when Paul set sail from Caesarea on an eventful journey that at first hugged the coasts of Syria, Cyprus and the Anatolian peninsula, until the whole company of 276 men arrived on the southern coast of Crete. From there they could try to hug the coast of Greece and cross over to Italy or face the open sea to cross WNW to Sicily and across the Straits of Messina into the Tyrrhenian Sea on to the port of Puteoli (Pozzuoli), and hence proceed to Rome. The prospect of facing the open Mediterranean in one of its deepest sections was a dangerous decision to make. It was late autumn and shipping lanes were officially closed because of the late autumn and winter storms. In spite of this, Julius, the centurion who was responsible to ferry the passengers on the large Alexandrian cargo ship, decided to follow the captain's decision to give it a try and make it to a safer harbour in Crete and winter there.

The decision was to prove disastrous. As soon as the ship rounded Cape Matala it met the fury of a strong ENE gale blowing down from Mount Ida (Psiloritis), the highest mountain in Crete. The ship was carried away towards the open sea, first in the direction of the islet of Gavdos (Cauda) and then on to the dreaded Syrtis Maior banks of Libya. In order to avoid catastrophe, the sailors and captain aptly turned the ship facing north and sideways to the gale, in order to be carried westwards. They had no inkling where they would end up. Maybe they were hoping to get to Sicily. After fourteen days of hell, the ship was dashed to pieces on a reef or sand shoal facing "a bay with a beach", in a place "where two seas meet" (διθάλασσον / *dithálasson*). Miraculously all the persons on board swam safe and sound to land. They had landed on an island, but they had no way of recognising its features. Welcomed kindly by the indigenous natives, they came to know that the island was called Μελίτη (*Melítē*).

This eventful journey is narrated by the evangelist Luke, author of the Acts of the Apostles, in chapters 27 and 28:1-10 of this book, in the style of a diary of navigation. Indeed, the narrative is the best-preserved example of navigational journeying in the Bible and maybe stands on a par with famous texts like Homer's Ὀδύσσεια (*Odýsseia*). The aim of Luke, however, is purely theological. He does not intend to present an expert description of a sea-journey, but rather to fit in the story within the overall plan of the Acts namely, that of proving how the Gospel of Jesus Christ was preached first in Jerusalem, then in Samaria, and finally, through the apostolic efforts of Paul of Tarsus, "to the ends of the earth." The journey to Rome was the coronation of such an effort, and the events narrated in chapters 27 and 28 of Acts are meant to be of service to the evangelisation of the gentiles, for which Paul merits pride of place and the title of Apostle.

To what island is Luke referring? *Melítē*, or *Mélita* in Latin, sounds familiar with the names of at least two islands in the Mediterranean basin. The most accepted theory is that it refers to the island of Malta, situated in the centre of the Mediterranean, 80 km south of Cape Passero in Sicily, 284 km east of Tunisia, and 333 km north of Libya. It is an archipelago covering 316 km^2, and consists essentially of three islands, namely Malta (*Maleth, Mélita, Malitah*), Gozo (Għawdex, *Gaulos/Gavdos*), and Comino (Kemmuna), and some other islets. Its coordinates are 35°54'N 14°31'E / 35.900°N 14.517°E. This means that the archipelago lies slightly WNW of the coordinates of the islet of Gavdos, off the southern coast of Crete (34.8462° N, 24.0845° E).

The other island with a similar name is Mljet (*Meleda*), in the Adriatic Sea, off the Dalmatian coast, NW of the city of Dubrovnik in modern day Croatia. It is 98.01 km^2, and its coordinates are 42.7478° N, 17.5150° E. This means that it lies much further north than Crete, in a NNW direction. To reach Mljet from Crete a ship would have to follow the Greek coast, hugging the island of Cephalonia (*Kephalonía*), and then entering the Adriatic through the Straits of Otranto.

Both islands have historically defended the honour of having welcomed the Apostle Paul on their shores. Both have their reasons for doing so. Malta lies across the route that Luke describes in Acts. The gale that brought Paul's ship to its shores is the typical *Gregale* storm that batters the island every autumn, bringing force 8 winds from the ENE, precisely from the direction of Crete. A meteorological examination of this gale shows a set pattern that recurs every time moist and warm air from Libya meets cold currents on Mount Ida in Crete, creating an intense area of low pressure moving away from the island in a westerly direction towards Tunisia. This cyclone is accompanied by strong wind and intense rainfall, which dampens the atmosphere and impairs visibility. This partly explains why the sailors could not recognise the land when they were approaching *Melítē*. When Paul arrived, Malta and Gozo were Roman *municipia*. The islands had fallen under Roman rule in 218 BC, initially under the praetorship of Sicily, but later on each island gained *municipium* status. This explains why there was a τῷ πρώτῳ τῆς νήσου, a "chief man" or *prōtos*, of the island, which the Acts name as Publius, who welcomed Paul and his companions in his estates and offered them hospitality for three days. Another interesting detail is that the natives are called οἵ τε βάρβαροι (*hoí te bárbaroi*), a word that is normally interpreted as referring to persons who could not speak Greek. Indeed, the Maltese natives spoke a Punic dialect, having been under Phoenician and Punic rule, but this, as we shall see, is not the only meaning of "barbarians". The last note regarding Malta is the mentioning of the ἔχιδνα (*échidna*), or viper, that was aroused by the heat of the fire and attached itself to Paul's hand when he was adding brushwood to the fire. In Malta there are no vipers, and the species of snakes living there are harmless. This is maybe one of the toughest hurdles to overcome in order to prove that Malta was indeed the scene of the shipwreck of the Apostle.

On the other hand, the island of Mljet was infested with highly poisonous snakes until 1910, when the snake population was brought under control. It is a very densely wooded island, in which snakes can live freely, and up till this very day is scantily populated. It also lies close to the Dalmatian coast, and it is an accepted fact that shipping lanes would normally hug the coast and not choose the open sea. A ship going from Greece to Italy could cross the Adriatic, and Mljet lies a relatively short distance north of the Straits of Otranto. The Adriatic is also the name given to the sea by Luke, who calls it "in the sea of *Adria* (Ἀδρίᾳ)." To what geographical extent of the sea is he referring? Is he simply speaking of the Adriatic Sea as we know it today? In antiquity, it seems that the Adriatic Sea extended way beyond the Straits of Otranto and would include the Adriatic Gulf (the modern Adriatic Sea where Mljet is situated) and the Sea of Adria, covering the entire expanse of water between the Peloponnese, Crete and Sicily. Not all agree with this thesis, advocated since classical times, and the defenders of Mljet have a strong argument to state that Paul was shipwrecked in the Adriatic and not in the *Mare Siculum*, or what is now known as Ionian Sea. Thus, they would speak of Mljet as the *Melita Illyrica*, as opposed to Malta, the *Melita Africana*. Moreover, the Adriatic also experiences a gale force wind from the SE, called *Jugo* in Croatian, which has the similar characteristics to the *Scirocco* wind in the Mediterranean or also to the *Gregale* wind we have already mentioned. Finally, the inhabitants of Mljet were Neretva settlers from the mainland, and they certainly were barbarians who could not speak Greek.

In the 18th century, the question regarding the authentic *Melítē* mentioned in Acts 28:1 reached its peak in the discussion between various authors, but especially after the publication of a study by a Croatian Benedictine abbot of the monastery of Saint Mary on Mljet, by the name of Ignjat Đurđević (Ignazio Giorgi) from Dubrovnik, who in 1730 published an erudite and voluminous work to prove that Mljet, and not Malta, was the place where Saint Paul was shipwrecked. His main thesis is that the cult towards Saint Paul on the island of Malta was more recent than that existing on Mljet, and that it was introduced and enhanced by the prestige and power of the Knights of the Order of Saint John, especially after 1610, when Grand Master Alof de Wignacourt proceeded to endow with great devotional value the so-called Grotto of Saint Paul in Rabat (where the ancient Roman town of *Melítē* stood) and the bay that was considered to be the place of the shipwreck of the Apostle, namely the *Cala di San Paolo*, where he built a church to commemorate the event. At the same time, Đurđević tried to ridicule many of the Maltese popular devotions towards Saint Paul, and to question their historical value, while enhancing the value of Mljet as the authentic spot where Paul was shipwrecked. His many arguments are strengthened by references to classical authors, by a scientific biblical interpretation of Acts 27-28 and especially by the testimony of the Byzantine Emperor Constantine Porphyrogenitus in his *De administrando imperio*.

Đurđević soon found an opponent to his thesis in the person of Giovanni Antonio Ciantar, a Maltese nobleman and scholar, who published his own answer to the Mljet theory in an equally detailed study in 1738, in defence of the Order of Saint John's interests in Malta and its efforts to promote the island as a devotional centre for the cult of Saint Paul. Ciantar's study, together with that of other eminent Maltese scholars, like Giovanni Francesco Abela and Giovanni Pietro Francesco Agius De Soldanis, tries to defend at all costs the value of Malta as the exact location mentioned in Acts, and as an island that can boast of having a Church with an apostolic foundation.

The so-called "shipwreck controversy", which was further complicated with the Cephalonia theory, has never been satisfactorily resolved, and maybe never will be. It is true, of course, that contemporary biblical exegesis and historical documentation all point to Malta as the place where Paul was shipwrecked. Yet, the Croatian tradition has never really died down. One has to remember that, if the Maltese theory was supported by the powerful influence of the Order of the Knights of Saint John, the Mljet/Meleda theory defended by Đurđević was also based upon the prestige of the famous city-state Republic of Ragusa, or Dubrovnik. During a time when the supremacy of the seas was being fought for by various European powers, and especially by the Republic of Venice, in perpetual war against the Ottoman Turks, but also with the safeguarding of commercial interests with the arch-enemy of the Christian religion, the importance of having been evangelised by the great Apostle Saint Paul was very significant in order to have a common denominator in the battle against Islam and in support of the Catholic Church. In both Ragusa and Malta the influence of the ecclesiastical establishment was supreme.

Our aim in this study is not that of providing a detailed analysis of the cult of Saint Paul in Malta. Many volumes have been published on this issue, containing studies by eminent scholars, many of whom are Maltese. In 2008-2009, when Pope Benedict XVI invited Christians worldwide to commemorate 2000 years since the birth of Paul of Tarsus, and again in 2010, when the Maltese celebrated 1950 years since the shipwreck of the Apostle, the interest on the figure of Saint Paul increased with symposiums, congresses, exhibitions, publications, etc. Although Malta had its fair share in such an effort, one cannot forget that a handful of scholars in Croatia also tried to foster the importance of the cult of Saint Paul in the area of Dubrovnik, also through scientific publications.

It was this interest and curiosity in the Mljet theory that prompted me to try to understand better the complexities of the whole controversy surrounding the shipwreck of Saint Paul. To do so I had to go personally to see and visit Mljet. With the kind generosity of a good Croatian brother and friend, Fr. Sandro Tomašević OFM, from the Franciscan Province of Zagreb, Croatia, who kindly accompanied me twice to Mljet and took the photos of this enchanting island, I was lucky to see my dream come true. Had it not been for his efforts, I would never have been able to visit Mljet so thoroughly. Obviously, since I am Maltese, I am not convinced with the Mljet theory. However, I believe that popular traditions are not born out of nothing, and that a grain of truth can be found in them. Mljet is no exception. It does not abound with Pauline memories and places of cult as Malta does, but the memory of Saint Paul on the island is ancient. There are some Byzantine and Mediaeval remains, just as there are many more in Malta. What one can conclude is that, while Malta is certainly the *Melítē* of Acts, the cult of Saint Paul in Dalmatia is also documented, or at least, hinted at, by references in the New Testament and in early Christian history. Unfortunately, both Malta and Mljet have no hard and fast archaeological or documentary evidence that goes back to the 1st century AD, and therefore the possibility of conjecture must be left open.

My plan in this work is simple. I first intend to analyse the treatise of Đurđević from the point of view of its contents, in order to provide a summary of what the Croatian abbot states regarding the core issues of the controversy, including the name *Melítē*, the Sea of Adria, the viper, the devotional value of Pauline memories in Malta. Đurđević also devotes particular attention to the beauty of the island of Mljet, where he lived in the monastery of Saint Mary on the western tip of the island. The enchanting monastery and church, which are still visible today, lie on a tiny island in the midst of what used to be a freshwater lake, later on transformed into a seawater lake when a channel was dug connecting it to the open sea.

The island itself will be the object of our second chapter, entitled "Otok Mljet", the Island of Mljet. This chapter will describe the island from the geographical and historical points of view, and also try to discover the few vestiges of cult to Saint Paul, which Đurđević presents as having roots in antiquity. My tour of the island also made me discover some possible locations where the supposed shipwreck could have taken place, particularly those which resemble a place "where two seas meet".

After having presented the Dalmatian island of Mljet, or *Melita Illyrica*, I will proceed to a parallel plan in the case of Malta, or *Melita Africana*. In chapter 3,

I will present a summary of the work by Giovanni Antonio Ciantar, which is an apologetic response to Đurđević's volume, constructed very much along the same lines. I will show how Ciantar tries to confute the theses of the Benedictine abbot, one by one, with proofs taken from the ancient traditions of Malta, which all point to a strong cult of Saint Paul in the various memories linked with catacombs, cave churches and mediaeval churches scattered throughout the island, as well as with place names that are associated with Paul and his physical presence in Malta.

Chapter 4 deals with the description of the *Gregale* gale that carried Paul to *Melítē*, and to the account of Acts 27, which deals with the minute details of the sea journey that brought Paul providentially to Malta. My aim is not that of providing an exegetical or theological reading of the account. This does not fall within my competence, and literature on the topic is abundant. It is rather my aim to provide a description of the meteorological phenomena associated with the *Gregale* gale and its influence on Malta, drawn also from my personal experience of this stormy weather that hits the Maltese islands nearly every year in late autumn or early winter. My aim is also that of pinpointing the various possible places on the Maltese coast where the shipwreck could have occurred, without arriving at any hard and fast conclusion, since archaeological evidence is lacking and we do not possess enough information as to the configuration of the geology of Malta nearly 2000 years ago. Having said this, it is interesting to note the close relationship between toponomy and devotion towards Saint Paul, which is not simply an "invention" of the Knights of Saint John, but goes back much further in time, and could be based on solid traditions.

The last chapter will dwell upon the cult of Saint Paul in Malta, describing how it can be constructed from the documentary evidence of the narrative of Acts 28:1-10, as well as from the various places that are witnesses of such a cult, including the traditional places associated with the shipwreck, the cave church known as Saint Paul's Grotto in Rabat, and other churches dedicated to the Apostle and marking possible locations where he would have preached and worked miracles on the island.

The cult of Saint Paul on Malta is unfortunately intertwined with many legendary elements that were the reason why a certain number of scholars dismissed the Malta story of the shipwreck of Paul as a myth. The truth, however, is that Malta has always been placed at the crossroads of cultures and dominated by various powers who ruled the Mediterranean. Even the ecclesiastical history of the island was seen as swinging between the influence of Byzantine Constantinople and Latin Rome. The Arab domination of the islands, officially dated to between 870 and 1090, further complicates matters. Nowadays, much light has been shed on historical truth with a scientific analysis of documentary material going back to the 12th century, through which we come to know that there was a Christian presence on the Maltese archipelago, particularly in Gozo.

The oldest reference to the shipwreck of Saint Paul on *Melítē* comes from Byzantine sources of the 10th century, as we shall see, and precisely from Constantine VII Porphyrogenitus in his *De administrando imperio*. This is the reason why Đurđević defends his stance on Mljet/Meleda with such strong arguments. The case of Malta was different. Even though Malta was certainly Christian from the 7th century onwards, and there are archaeological vestiges of a Christian presence way back in the 4th century, the fact that the island had been under Arab Muslim control did not help at all to foster its Christian identity. According to an expert Maltese historian, "in the twelfth century, Malta was largely Muslim. A few years earlier, in 1175, Burchard Bishop of Strassburg, who presumably had stopped on the island while on his way on an embassy to Egypt had described it as *'a Sarracenis inhabitata'*."[1] The Maltese spoke a language like that of the Saracens. Hence the possible confusion. The Normans had definitely conquered the Maltese archipelago by 1127 and had embarked upon a Christianisation and Latinisation process on the local population.

In spite of this undeniable historical truth, the fact that Malta's links with Saint Paul have been so strong is an indication that the memory of the Apostle on the island was alive for many centuries. Even if one ignores the false fabrications of history that should justly be dismissed, the mythological element of Paul's presence is not without a historical foundation, based as it is on a narrative that comes from the pen of the evangelist Luke of Antioch, who accompanied Paul on his eventful journey to Rome. If Malta was truly the island in which Paul was welcomed after his shipwreck, and where he stayed for three months in A.D. 60-61, then it comes as natural to think and reason about his activity on *Melítē* within the parametres of what we come to know from the same Book of Acts regarding his activity in many other places which he visited in his apostolic journeys.

In other words, what I am trying to state is simply that Paul did leave a flourishing Christian community on *Melítē* just as he did in many other places that he evangelised. This does not mean that we can speculate about the composition of such a community and make of it a well-organised ecclesiastical establishment modelled upon the Tridentine notion of hierarchy. Unfortunately, this mistake was made by the eminent Maltese historians who, during the 17th century, wanted at all costs to defend the uninterrupted apostolic succession of the local hierarchy and its direct link to Paul's mission. It is not necessary to go so far in order to prove, with some common sense, that Paul did land on *Melita Africana*, as Đurđević would have it, and that he did leave a Christian legacy of some sort, just as he would have done had he truly landed on *Melita Illyrica* at some stage of his later life and

---

[1] M. Buhagiar, (2006), 159. Except in the case of the sources, the other studies listed in the bibliography will be quoted with the author's name, date of publication and page.

mission, maybe after his release from the Roman capitivity. This, however, goes beyond the scope of the author of Acts, as well as beyond the scope of our present analysis.

In my work I have found invaluable and expert help from Professor Chev. Horatio Caesar Roger Vella. He not only offered me many suggestions and read through my work with painstaking patience in order to note corrections, but he also volunteered to write the preface for this book. I personally feel privileged to have found in him an expert scholar and a good friend, and I will ever be grateful and indebted to him.

Although I have personally written this study, I expressly wished to include the name of my Franciscan brother Sandro Tomašević as the co-author. As I have already stated, without him it would not have been possible for me to visit Dubrovnik and especially the enchanting island of Mljet. I thank him for his photos of the island and for his fraternal patience in accompanying me during my visits to *Melita Illyrica* in order to discover traces of traditions linked to Saint Paul's shipwreck, just as there are in my island home of *Melita Africana*. Two islands with one name, but also with one tradition of having welcomed the Apostle of the Gentiles. That is why this book is entitled: *Melita Illyrica* and *Melita Africana*: The Islands of Saint Paul.

Chapter 1

Ignjat Đurđević and the Mljet theory of Saint Paul's shipwreck

The Saint Paul's shipwreck controversy was ignited by a Benedictine monk from Dubrovnik (Ragusa) in 1730, Ignjat Đurđević (Ignazio Giorgi), who wrote an erudite study claiming that Saint Paul was shipwrecked on the coast of the island of Mljet (Meleda) in the Adriatic, off the coast of Dubrovnik.[2] The volume is an interesting and scholarly representation of the author's theory, and merits a special attention because of the importance that the question of the location of Paul's shipwreck assumed at that particular historical moment. My aim is that of presenting a summary of Đurđević's volume, after a reading of its contents and also with the help of my personal observations upon visiting twice the island of Mljet.

Ignjat Đurđević

Ignjat Đurdević[3] was born in Dubrovnik (Ragusa), the famous Republic on the Dalmatian coast, in 1675, son of Bernard Đurđević and Teresa Zlatarić. His baptismal name was Nikola (Nicolò). He came from the noble Giorgi (Đurđević) family, which received its title of nobility after the earthquake of 1667.

---

[2] Ignjat Đurđević, *Divus Paulus Apostolus in mari, quod nunc Ventus sinus dicitur, naufragus et Melitae Dalmatensis insulae post naufragium hospes sive de genuino significatu duorum locorum in Actibus Apostolicis.* Cap. XXVII,27. Navigantibus nobis in Adria. Cap. XXVIII,1. Tunc cognovimus quia Melita insula vocabatur. Inspectiones anticriticae auctore D. Ignatio Georgio, Benedictino e congregatione Melitensi Ragusina. Adjicitur brevis Dissertatio eiudem Auctoris de Catellis Melitacis. Venetiis, apud Gristophorum Zane Superiorum permissum, ac privilegio, MDCCXXX.

This volume has been edited into Croatian, with an introduction in English, by Miho Demović (2008), Zagreb. (Ignat Đurđević's 1730 book translated from elite Latin into Croatian by Jozo Marević, with forward by Dr. Miho Demović in Croatian and English). Another study in Croatian on the same theme is that by Zlatko Pavetić (ed.) (2015), Zagreb.

[3] Gliubich S. (1856), 145-150.

Nikola spent his youthful years living a comfortable and often reckless life. He was chosen for the position of Duke of Šipan, but lost his title because of his excessive love adventures, especially toward an unknown young female from Dubrovnik, after he addressed a love-poem to her that was deemed libertine.

He was an erudite poet, having received his education with the Jesuits of Dubrovnik, and studied philosophy under Luka Kodrić. He could write in Latin, Italian and Croatian, and became famous for his *Ljuvene pjesni*, or love poems. His most famous work was entitled *Uzdasi Mandaljene pokornice* (*Sighs of Repentant Magdalene*), printed in Venice in 1728. In 1729, he also published a volume of paraphrases of the Psalms entitled *Saltijer Slovinski* (*Slavic Psalms*).

In 1697, when he was 22, Nikola went to Rome and there he entered the Jesuit Society. He continued to study Theology and the other arts and sciences, as well as Biblical Hebrew. His superiors sent him to Ascoli as lecturer of Rhetoric. He remained as a Jesuit for eight years, but his frail health compelled him to leave the Society and return to his hometown Dubrovnik, where in 1705, when he was 30, he joined the Benedictine monastic Order and changed his name to Ignjat (Ignazio). He entered the Benedictine Congregation of Meleda, which existed in the Republic of Ragusa, and particularly on the island of Mljet, where Ignjat became a member, and also Abbot, of the community of the monastery of Otočić Sveta Marija (Saint Mary) on the islet in the Veliko Jezero (Big Lake) on the north-west corner of the island. The Benedictines had arrived in Mljet from Monte Gargano and Pulsano in the Puglie region of Italy. They became feudal lords of the island in 1151. In 1187-1198, the Serbian Prince Desa of the House of Vojislavljević built for them the church and monastery of Saint Mary, on Veliko Jezero. Pope Innocent III recognised this foundation in 1198. The monastery was the centre of the *Congregatio Melitensis* or *Melitana*, the Mljet Congregation to which all Benedictine monks of the Republic of Ragusa belonged. The Benedictines remained feudal lords of Mljet until 1345 and then retained only a third of the island, which became part of the Republic of Ragusa in 1410. The monastery was abandoned in 1809, during the times of the Napoleonic wars, and the Seat of the Congregation moved to Sveti Jakov near Ragusa. In the 20th century the monastery and church were given over to the Bishop of Dubrovnik. The building became a hotel in 1960, but in 1998 it was returned to the Bishop.

In the period he lived as a Benedictine monk, Ignjat also occupied other prestigious offices. The Senate of Ragusa chose him as Councillor and Theologian of the Republic; he was one of the leaders of the Academy "degli Oziosi". He refused the bishopric of Trebinje in Herzegovina, which was repeatedly offered to him. He had travelled widely also in Italy, particularly in Naples and Padua, and kept constant correspondence with intellectuals of his times. For a period he entered into a bitter conflict with the civil authorities of Dubrovnik on the question of ecclesiastical immunity, and was exiled to Italy, where he visited many cities of the ancient Magna Græcia, until the Pope interceded for him and he could return to the Republic of Dubrovnik.

Ignjat Đurđević died on 12 January 1737, aged 61, after an apoplexy that he suffered in the house of his friend Raimondo Tudisio. He was buried in the monastery church of Sveti Jakov outside Dubrovnik. His contribution to Croatian literature as a baroque poet remains a strong element of his fame, but for us his polemical work on the shipwreck site of Saint Paul is of particular interest.

Divus Paulus Apostolus in mari. Đurđević's Theory on Saint Paul's Shipwreck on the Island of Mljet

The title of Ignjat Đurđević's volume in English reads: "Saint Paul the Apostle Shipwrecked in the Sea today called Venetian gulf, guest of the Dalmatian Island of Mljet after the shipwreck, or on the genuine significance of the two texts in the Acts of the Apostles, chapter XXVII,27: 'We were being driven here and there in the Sea of Adria,' and chapter XXVIII,28: "We came to know that the name of the island was Melita.'" The volume is meant to be a critical discussion of the whole issue, and is a strenuous attempt to defend the theory that the island of Mljet in the Adriatic (*Melita Illyrica*), and not the island of Malta (*Melita Africana*) was the site of Saint Paul's shipwreck. A good description of the contents of this volume has already been given by Miho Demović and has been published in English under the title: "A Study Accompanying Croatian Translation of the Đurđević's Book on Saint Paul's Shipwreck on the Island of Mljet."[4]

Ignjat Đurđević presents first a solemn dedication for his study, which he addresses to his erudite friends in Padua. The reason for doing so and avoiding to mention the citizens of Dubrovnik lay in the fact that such an action would have created political tension between the Republic of Ragusa and the Knights of Saint John, who at the time were feudal lords of Malta (1530-1798). The author prefers to address his dedication to persons living in the Republic of Venice, since it obviously had political and commercial interests in the Adriatic. As was customary at the time, the book had to receive the official *imprimatur* from an Inquisitor, and it did so on 19 February 1729, when the Inquisitor Toma Maria Gennari declared it free from doctrinal errors.

[4] This section forms the forward by Demović (2008) (Ignat Đurđević's 1730 book translated from elite Latin into Croatian by Jozo Marević, with forward by Dr. Miho Demović in Croatian and English), and can be downloaded from the website: www.croatianhistory.net (accessed 5 April 2017).

The synoptic analysis of Acts 27-28

Đurđević presents, first and foremost, a synoptic analysis of the two chapters 27 and 28 of the Book of the Acts of the Apostles, which deal respectively with the storm that brought Saint Paul to be shipwrecked on the shores of *Melítē* and the welcome that the Apostle received from the indigenous inhabitants of the island.

The method followed by Đurđević is that of listing on parallel columns the Vulgate Latin edition, the original Greek text of Luke's account, and then his own personal translation. By doing so he wanted to underline some important differences which, according to his scholarly methodology, were fundamental in proving his thesis that the island mentioned in the Acts of the Apostles is *Melita Illyrica* (Mljet) and not *Melita Africana* (Malta).

The main divergencies, according to Đurđević, concern the following terms: (1) the hurricane wind described in the Greek text is called Ευροκλύδων (*Euroklydōn*), which Saint Jerome in the Vulgate translates as *Euroaquilo*, when in truth it should retain its original Greek name *Euroklydōn*;[5] (2) the name of the Sea in which the ship was being tossed by the tempest is Αδρία, *Adria*, which according to Đurđević refers specifically to the Adriatic Sea (Venetian Gulf) and not to the outer open Sea which should, instead, be known as the Ionian Sea or Sicilian Sea; (3) the place of the shipwreck is indicated by the Greek word διθάλασσον, which the Vulgate translates as *in locum dithalassum*, whereas Đurđević translates as *in locum bimarem* (a place between two Seas); (4) the name of the island according to the Greek text is ὅτι Μελίτη, which the Vulgate translates as *Melita insula*, whereas Đurđević translates into *Melítē insula*; (5) the local indigenous inhabitants of the island are described as οἵ τε βάρβαροι in the Greek text, whereas the Latin of the Vulgate and Đurđević himself call them *Barbari*, indicating that the inhabitants of *Melítē/ Mélita* did not speak Greek or Latin. Đurđević insists that in *Melita Africana* Greek was spoken along with Punic, but not on *Melita Illyrica*; (6) the Apostle was bitten by an ἔχιδνα, *vipera*, or viper, and should surely have died because of its poisonous bite. Now on *Melita Illyrica* (Mljet) there are venomous vipers, but not on *Melita Africana* (Malta); (7) the prince or governor of the island is called τῷ πρώτῳ τῆς νήσου ὀνόματι Ποπλίῳ, translated in the Vulgate *principis insulae, nomine Publii*, and by Đurđević *primatem (seu principem) insulae, nomine Publium*. Who was this "prince"? Đurđević rejects the theory on *Melita Africana* that Publius was baptised by Paul and became the first bishop of the island.[6]

---

[5] Acts 27:14 according to Đurđević: *Post non multum autem jecit (se) contra ipsam ventus Typhonicus, appellatus Euroclydon.*

[6] Đurđević is correct. The Bishop Publius, as we shall see, existed elsewhere. Publius, the Governor (not Prince) of the island was probably baptised after the miracle performed on his father. *Prōtos* means chief man. The Latin equivalent is *Princeps*, but it cannot be translated as "prince."

Besides these indications, Đurđević also concludes that many of the Maltese traditions on *Melita Africana* referring to Paul's presence on the island are totally without any historical foundation. We shall take a look at the various contents of Đurđević's volume, which is divided into eight chapters. Before doing so, however, we shall examine the description that Đurđević gives of the island of Mljet, which is very interesting and detailed. We shall limit ourselves to Đurđević's own observations, and reserve a separate chapter for our personal presentation of modern day Mljet and its topographical, geographical and historical links with the tradition of the shipwreck of Saint Paul.

Đurđević's description of the Island of Mljet

> "The island of Melita, nowadays known as Meleda, lies in the Adriatic Sea, which we recently know by the name of Venetian Gulf. The supreme dominion over this Sea is held by the Republic of Ragusa, in which one also finds the Order of the Black Monks of Saint Benedict, or the Congregation that takes its name from the same island. On its western side one finds the island of Korčula (Korkyra Melaina, Corcyra Nigra), and on its eastern side the island of Šipan [...] on its outer shore it overlooks the coast of Italy, namely the mountain of Gargano in Puglia, from which it is less than one hundred and twenty miles distant. It is about three thousand feet from the Illyrian continent, and sixty miles from Epidaurum (Cavtat, Dalmatia): it is more than sixty miles in circumference, and it has five excellent and sheltered harbours, which are useful for big vessels. It is characterised by high mountains, fertile fields, pastures, and very dense forests, in which there are Vipers or Snakes, which to this very day have an instantaneous poison, in such a way that whoever is bitten by them, after a short while swells up, becomes pale, and dies there and then, just as the inhabitants of Melita thought of the Apostle Paul, when they said that he would swell up and drop dead immediately. The major part of the island, which overlooks the Sea, is full of jagged rocks and cliffs, and it is surrounded by them in such a way that to this day gently sloping shores are lacking, and there is more than one *dithalassos* (shoal, sandbank, underwater rock?); these are hidden underwater and are of great danger for shipping."[7]

This brief geographical description is an indication of the great familiarity which Đurđević had with the island of Mljet. In this section of his study he continues with such clear descriptions, with the aim of proving his thesis that Saint Paul was shipwrecked on the shores of Mljet.

Đurđević calls the inhabitants of Mljet *incolae simplices ac rudes, sed perquam hospitales*, simple and rustic inhabitants, but very hospitable. They must have been numerous when Saint Paul was shipwrecked on the island, but the incursions of other barbaric tribes and the tyranny of the Turkish invasions were the reason why the island was scantily populated in later historical periods. The author then delves

---

[7] Đurđević (1730), 32.

into the island's long history, particularly the war of Emperor Augustus against the people from Neretva, Korčula and Mljet in 35 B.C.

He mentions the port of Polače on the north coast of the island, where there are remains of a Roman palace and gate. The author refers to it as a *magnificum aedium [Palatium hodie vocant]*, hence the Croatian name Polače.

According to Đurđević, the island of Mljet is also famous because of its links with the nymph Calypso in Homer's *Odyssey*. He defends the thesis that the island of Ogygia and the cliff and cave of Calypso are to be found on *Melita Illyrica* and not on *Melita Africana* as other authors insisted during his times, particularly the Maltese historian of the Order of Saint John, Giovanni Francesco Abela (1582-1665).

He then mentions the Byzantine emperor Constantine Porphyrogenitus (909--959), who mentioned the island of Mljet in his *De Administrando Imperio*, and who came out with the theory that the island of *Melítē* mentioned in the Acts by Luke was that of Mljet in the Adriatic.[8]

Đurđević mentions the existence of an ancient town on Mljet that was destroyed during his times. He refers to a town known as the *Melitussa* of Illyria mentioned by Polybius.[9]

The most enchanting section of Đurđević's description of Mljet is the paragraph he dedicates to the description of the Veliko Jezero on which the Otočić Sveta Marija with the Benedictine monastery is situated:

> "In that same lake there is a tiny island, which is very beautiful and has a circular form, on which lies the monastery of our Congregation, built sturdily and fortified [...] In the Monastery church is venerated a painting of the Mother of God, which is known for its marvellous devotion not only by the Dalmatians [...]. Together with other visitors here came the son of King Toma of Bosnia, who died in this place and was buried in the sanctuary of the Virgin."[10]

Đurđević also refers to the southern section of the island, which lies on the extreme end facing SE. It is in this area, as we shall see later on, that there are the remains of an ancient church dedicated to Saint Paul close to the hamlet of Korita. In this same section of the coast are the two islets near Salpunara, which could mark the famous *bimare* site of Saint Paul's shipwreck according to Đurđević's theory.

Finally the author mentions various scholars and writers who mentioned Mljet by various names, among which *Melitene, Melitine, Meleta, Melta, Meligene,*

---

[8] Constantine Porphyrogenitus, *De Administrando Imperio*, 36. English translation by R.J.H. Jenkins, (1985^2), 164-165: "In Pagania are the inhabited cities of Mokron, Beroullia, Ostrok and Slavinetza. Also, they possess these islands: the large island of Kourkra, or Kiker, on which there is a city; another large island, Meleta, or Malozeatai, which Saint Luke mentions in the 'Acts of the Apostles' by the name of Melite, in which a viper fastened upon Saint Paul by his finger, and Saint Paul burnt it up in the fire."

[9] Μελίτουσσα, πόλις Ἰλλυρίας. POLYBIUS, *The Histories*, Vol. 4, Book XIII, Loebb Classical Library, Harvard 1925, revised 2011, 477.

[10] Đurđević (1730), 36.

Mitylene. Maybe it was the great confusion that these various names introduced that gave rise to the discussion as to which island refers Saint Luke in the Acts when he mentions *Melítē*, normally translated as Malta (called *Melita Africana* by Đurđević), but referring also, according to the same Đurđević, to Mljet (or *Melita Illyrica*), as well as being confused with other places having similar names, such as Miletus in modern Turkey and Mytilene on the island of Lesbos.

It is interesting to note that, besides Mljet, another place which boasts of the possibility that Saint Paul was shipwrecked on its shores is the Greek island of Cephalonia, where there is also a tiny church dedicated to the Apostle at Pessada, south of the port of Argostolion.

After a summary of the contents of his study, and an excursus on various authors consulted by Đurđević, which includes a staggering list, the author delves into the main topics related to his theme, basing his arguments on eight particular topics, to which he dedicates a chapter each. We shall here present a summary of the contents of these chapters.

Chapter 1: On the theories of the Philomaltenses and Philodalmatæ

As we have seen, the authors consulted by Đurđević comprised a group who were favourable to the *Melita Africana* theory, and another more numerous group, who opted for the *Melita Illyrica*. The author calls them respectively *Philomaltenses* and *Philodalmatæ*. Đurđević attempts to present the ridiculous assertions of the *Philomaltenses*, who he regards as having fabricated their theories without any scientific proof. Among the various false theories of the *Philomaltenses*, Đurđević mentions the following.

The first false theory regards the fact that the *Philomaltenses* believed that Saint Paul took the venom from the Maltese viper, thus making it innocuous, and that the soil of Malta had curative properties. A second false theory regards the geographical position of *Melítē*, which these false scholars placed between Epirus and Italy, to the point that they stated that Saint Paul was shipwrecked in the Adriatic and then swam to *Melita Africana*. A third confusion regards the name of the islet of Cauda, off Crete. Its Greek name is *Gavdos*, and these authors confuse it with the *Gaudos* of Malta, namely the island of Gozo.[11] They also mix Cape Salmone, which is situated in southern Crete, with an area in Saint Paul's Bay in Malta, which in Maltese is

---

[11] The name *Gaudos* originally belongs to the small island of *Gavdos*, lying to the southwest of the island of Crete, and called *Cauda* by Luke in Acts 27:16. Strabo also called the island of Gozo by the name of *Gaudos*, whereas its original name was *Gaulos*. From *Gaudos* derives the Maltese name *Għawdex*, by which Gozo is known. The question of the name of *Gaudos* has been studied by Prof. H.C.R. Vella (2012), 2-20.

called Selmun, (Italianized in the surname Salomone and Maltizised into Selmun), and which overlooks the islet which is traditionally considered as one of the possible places of Saint Paul's shipwreck on the island of Malta.[12] The *Philomaltenses* claimed that Malta had many good harbours, whereas Meleda in the Adriatic did not have any harbours in which ships could winter. Another false theory regards the consecration of the Roman governor of Malta, Publius, as bishop of the island, after he had been converted to Christianity by Saint Paul. They state that the provincial council of Miletus (*Concilio Melivetano*) of 416 against Pelagius was celebrated in *Melita Africana*, and that the ancient troglodyte church of the *Madonna tal-Mellieħa* in Malta was consecrated by the bishops who attended the council. The legend of the nymph Calypso is also transferred from its correct location in Mljet to a cave in Gozo, which has erroneously been considered to be the island of Ogygia. The *Philomaltesnes* also mix the ancient history of Mljet with that of Malta when they describe the Roman wars against the inhabitants of Neretva.

Đurđević was certainly correct in many of his critical arguments against the *Philomaltenses*, since many of these theories were, in fact, false, or were made up in order to enhance the cult of Saint Paul on the island of Malta during the reign of the Knights of Saint John. Obviously, these arguments are of no help in opting for or against the island of Mljet in the Adriatic since, as we shall see, there are other factors one has to bear in mind. Đurđević, in fact, was aware of this, and that is why he delves into a thorough analysis of other issues such as the climatic factor of the hurricane wind that brought Saint Paul to the island of *Melítē*.

Chapter 2: On the Sea of Adria

The issue of the name of the Sea in which Saint Paul was shipwrecked is crucial to Đurđević. In Acts 27:27 Saint Luke writes: Ὡς δὲ τεσσαρεσκαιδεκάτη νὺξ ἐγένετο διαφερομένων ἡμῶν ἐν τῷ Ἀδρίᾳ, which is normally translated as: "And when the fourteenth night came on, while we were being driven one way and another in the Adriatic." The whole issue hinges upon the geographical limits of the "Sea of Adria," or simply, "Adriatic." Modern maps are quite clear about the extent of the Adriatic Sea, in which the island of Mljet is found, placing its extension from the Gulf of Venice in the north to the Straits of Otranto in the south. Đurđević insists upon calling this Sea as *Sinus Veneti*, or the Venetian Gulf, and defends the thesis that the Adriatic Sea includes only this specific geographical extension. On the other hand, various authors in antiquity have called by the name Adria a

[12] The islet of Saint Paul, where there is the statue of the apostle indicating it as the site of the shipwreck, is also known by the name of Selmunett, since it just out from the cliff face of the Selmun promontory. It was named after Saint Paul only in 1960.

much larger extension of Sea, covering much of what is commonly known as the Ionian Sea, between the island of Crete and Sicily, and extending as far south as the Syrtis Banks on the northern coast of Africa. The importance of such an issue is crucial for Đurđević, since he bases his defence of Mljet as the island of Paul's shipwreck upon it, and finds his principal argument against Malta as being the island of the shipwreck, since it is found in the Libyan Sea, or Sicilian Sea, or simply Mediterranean, very far from the geographical limits of the Adriatic.

According to Đurđević, it was Ptolemy (100 – 170) who created the confusion, since he stretched the boundaries of the Adriatic to what is currently the Ionian Sea on the east of Sicily. The *Philomaltenses* continued to extend this area to include the extent of Sea further south between Sicily and Africa, where *Melita Africana* is situated. Thus they could assert that Malta was to be found in the Adriatic Sea. It has to be remembered, however, that the Acts never state that *Melítē* was situated in the Adriatric.

The great merit of Đurđević is that he quotes various authors to defend his thesis. He particularly quotes the geographer Strabo (64 B.C. – 21 A.D.), who aptly described the Mediterranean as a collection of various seas, including the Iberian Sea, outside the coast of Spain; the Ligurian Sea, outside the southern French and Italian coast; the Sardinian Sea, between the island of Sardinia and Africa; the Tyrrhenean Sea, between Italy and Sicily; the Sicilian (*Sikelikon*) Sea between Sicily and the Peloponnese (the current Ionian Sea); the Adriatic-Ionian (*Adrias – Jonium*) Sea between Italy and Dalmatia; the Aegean Sea, between Greece and Turkey; the Cretan Sea, between Crete and Greece; the Sea of Pamphylia, between Cyprus and Asia Minor; the Egyptian Sea, outside the coast of Egypt; and the Libyan Sea, outside the coast of Libya. According to Đurđević, Strabo was very clear regarding the extent of the Adriatic Sea and that of the Sicilian Sea (*Mare Siculum et Mare Ausonium*). Since his analysis predated that of Claudius Ptolemy, one should give it pride of place in his ability to distinguish in precision the extent of the various seas in the Mediterranean.

Đurđević quotes many other authors who defend Strabo's thesis and strengthen his position that the Adriatic was circumscribed within the boundaries of the present sea between Italy and Dalmatia, having as its natural boundary the Straits of Otranto. He is especially careful to point out that Saint Luke could not possibly have erred in his reference to the Sea of Adria, since he wrote the Acts of the Apostles before the appearance of Claudius Ptolemy, when it was fairly clear that the Sea of Adria referred explicitly to the Adriatic and not to its subsequent extension southwards in the Sicilian Sea.[13]

---

[13] However, one should state that Ptolemy (c. 100 – c. 168 A.D.) did not invent his assertion regarding the extent of the Adriatic. He was following a common understanding also known to Luke, the author of the Acts, who wrote the shipwreck account just a few decades before.

Luke's expertise in geographical analysis, according to Đurđević, is proved by the fact that he knew about Paul's plans to visit Nicopolis, as described in Titus 3:12: "As soon as I have sent Artemas or Tychicus to you, do your best to join me at Nicopolis, where I have decided to spend the winter." Now Nicopolis is situated in the Greek peninsula of Preveza, which lies south of Corfù, nearly at the entrance to the Adriatic Sea. Hence, Paul would have known that the Adriatic referred explicitly to that stretch of sea that separated Italy from Dalmatia.

Chapter 3: On the Viper of *Melítē*

Another important issue raised by Đurđević regards the venomous viper that bit Paul on the island of *Melítē*. The Acts state that the inhabitants of the island expected to see Paul fall down dead as a result of the deadly poison in the viper, but then nothing of the sort happened, and Paul just shook the viper into the fire and suffered no harm. According to the *Philomaltenses*, this miracle was evident in the fact that, on the island of *Melita Africana* there are no poisonous snakes, for the simple reason that Paul took away their deadly substance through divine intervention. Moreover, even the same soil and earth of Malta acquired curative properties as a result of this miracle. Đurđević dismisses all these traditons as pious inventions, and states that *Melita Illyrica*, that is, the island of Mljet in the Adriatic, is full of poisonous vipers, and that is one of the greatest proofs that Paul was shipwrecked on this island and not on Malta.

The simple explanation provided by Đurđević has, indeed, its weight of significance, at least taken at face value, since it is true that there are no poisonous snakes in Malta, even though we are not sure whether there were any at the time Paul arrived on the island. Đurđević shows how ridiculous the Maltese traditions were, namely those that were born at the place where Paul was supposed to have been kept imprisoned when he was wintering on Malta. The place is known as Saint Paul's Grotto in Rabat, just outside the walls of the ancient Roman town of *Melítē* (nowadays, Mdina). Fragments of the rock of this grotto were sent all over Europe, especially during the period in which Malta was governed by the Order of Saint John, since these pieces of rock were reputed to contain miraculous power against snake venom. Another fake tradition, according to Đurđević, regarded the export of local Maltese fossils, the snake-like fossils or shark teeth belonging to the extinct monaster shark "Charcarocles megalodon" which used to live in the Tethys ocean, and which are sometimes found embedded in the local Maltese Globigerina limestone outcrops on the coast of the island. They resemble tongues, and in fact, in Maltese they are known as "Ilsien San Pawl" (the tongue of Saint Paul), because of the presumed miraculous properties they were believed to hold.

In order to prove his thesis that the story of the curative properties of Maltese soil were all made up, and that the true venomous vipers were to be found on Mljet and not on Malta, Đurđević sent some very poisonous vipers from Mljet to a physician of Padua, by the name Antonio Vallisneri, and asked him to make experiments with their poison to see and prove how effective it was to kill a person. At the end of this chapter, Đurđević presents a long letter by Vallisneri, who replied to his queries by showing how he had used these vipers on some poor domestic animals in order to see the effect the poison could exert on these unfortunate creatures! In this way Đurđević continued to prove his assertion that it was Mljet the island of the shipwreck, since during his times it was infested by vipers. During the 20th century, Asian mongooses were introduced on the island, and they nearly completely wiped out the viper population of Mljet.[14]

Chapter 4: On the Barbarians of *Melítē*

In Acts 28:2, Luke mentions the inhabitants of *Melítē* by the name οἵ τε βάρβαροι, an expression which is roughly translated by the term "inhabitants", but which literally means "barbarians." The term refers to races which could not speak the classical languages, namely Greek or Latin. In other words, in order to prove that *Melita Africana* or *Melita Illyrica* were the place where the apostle was shipwrecked, and where he was kindly received by the Barbarian inhabitants, one needs to prove which one of the two islands housed a population which could not speak either one of the two classical languages.

According to Đurđević the inhabitants of *Melita Africana* were not Barbarians during the time when Paul was shipwrecked. They were Hellenized and were inhabitants of a Roman *municipium*. So, they should have known Greek and Latin, and thus cannot be described as being Barbarians.[15] The inhabitants of *Melita Illyrica,* or Mljet, on the other hand, were native tribes of Neretva and Korčula, who practised piracy on Roman ships in the Adriatic, and had to be subdued by emperor

---

14 For a detailed analysis of the viper species that are present on Mljet, and which were certainly more numerous in Đurđević's times, see D. Jelić, I. Budinski, B. Lauš (2012), 165-178. The venomous viper which is endemic on Mljet is the *Vipera ammodytes ammoditytes*, or Nose-horned Viper, which was reported to be present in huge numbers on Mljet until 1908, but which became exceptionally rare by 1927 because of the Small Indian Mongoose (*Herpestes auropunctatus*) introduced on Mljet in 1910, which practically wiped out the viper population. According to these scientists, some species might still be present in the more inaccessible parts in higher elevations of the island: http://www.zobodat.at/pdf/HER_24_3_4_0165-0178.pdf (accessed 20 May 2017).

15 The Maltese natives knew Greek as well as Punic. A few of them might also have known Latin as a foreign language.

Augustus in 35 B.C. This is another proof that Saint Paul and his shipwrecked companions were kindly received by the Barbarian inhabitants of Mljet, and not by the inhabitants of Malta.

This thesis by Đurđević has a certain intrinsic value, but it should be seen against the backdrop of the true history of Malta during the time when Paul was shipwrecked. Malta had been occupied by the Romans in 218 B.C. At the time, it was made up of a peaceful coalition between Phoenician/Punic and Greek races. So, although it is true that Malta was Hellenized when Paul arrived, it is also true that Punic influences were very strong, and that Phoenician was normally spoken in Malta. In this way, the term Barbarians could very well fit the description of the native Maltese, even because of another thesis that delves into the authentic meaning of the word *barbaroi* in Greek, deriving it from Oriental languages which used the term *bar* to refer to peasants or farmers, as well as the same term *bar* to refer to their descendants, that is, "children of the countryside."[16]

Chapter 5: On the Typhonic Gale

We have already noted that the gale which brought Paul to the shores of *Melítē* is called Ευροκλύδων (Euroklydōn) in Acts 27:14, but that it has often been interpreted as being Ευρακύλων (Eurakylōn), translated by Saint Jerome as *Euroaquilo*. The same Vulgate calls the gale by the name "ventus typhonicus", which means a strong gale, or even hurricane.

It is not our intention at this point to enter into the detailed analysis of this particular gale-force wind. We shall limit ourselves to what Đurđević himself states in defence of his position that the gale that brought Paul ashore on Melite led his ship not on *Melita Africana* but on *Melita Illyrica.*

A cursory glance at a map of the Mediterranean shows the complexity of such an affirmation, since the direction from Crete to Malta is radically different to that from Crete to Mljet. Đurđević defends the position that the Euroklydōn gale refers to a strong wind blowing in a south-easterly direction, whereas the Eurakylōn blows rather in a north-easterly direction. If we see the coordinates of Mljet and Malta respectively from Cape Matala in Crete, where the gale originated, we notice that a SE direction would have blown the ship roughly towards the entrance to the Adriatic and on to Mljet, even though it would have been a SSE gale that could achieve such an end, whereas a NE gale would have blown it on the Syrtis Banks in Libya, and it would have to be an ENE gale that would be able to blow it to the

[16] H.C.R. Vella (2012), 7-8, quotes the Maltese linguist Mikiel Anton Vassalli (1764-1829), who gave such an interpretation to the Greek word Βάρβαροι.

shores of Malta. One could reason that the gale was a Levanter wind without any specification of the exact direction where it was blowing. We shall see that the issue can be satisfactorily resoved on a meteorological level, but this would take us out of Đurđević's analysis and his concrete possibilities of research in the 18th century.

Đurđević is adamant in defending the term *Euroklydōn*, and in stating that it was a SE gale that carried Paul's ship into the Adriatic and on to Mljet. He proves his assertion by stating that, in the Adriatic, the only two gale-force winds are the Bora, or Bura (in Croatian) N or NE katabatic wind blowing from the Dinaric Alps, which hits the Dalmatian coast in violent icy gusts, and the Jugo, or SE humid and warm gale that blows for days on end on the Dalmatian coast. The other winds are not so strong, namely the Mistral, or NW wind, and the Libeccio, or SW wind. In any case, the only wind that could bring a vessel into the Adriatic through the Straits of Otranto is the Jugo or any Levanter strong gale. Đurđević states that this climatic phenomenon is not rare, and that the direction it takes in the Adriatic blows a ship directly upon Mljet. Indeed, the place where the shipwreck is reputed to have taken place on Mljet lies on the SE extremity of the island, at Saplunara, close to Korita, and in the straits between Mljet and the islets of Veliki Školj and Mali Školj.[17]

Chapter 6: On Publius the Melitean

According to Acts 28:7: Ἐν δὲ τοῖς περὶ τὸν τόπον ἐκεῖνον ὑπῆρχεν χωρία τῷ πρώτῳ τῆς νήσου ὀνόματι Ποπλίῳ (In the areas around that place there were estates belonging to the chief man of the island, by name Publius). The title given to Publius by Luke is *prōtos*, translated as "the chief man" (of the island) and as *princeps insulae* in the Vulgate edition. Đurđević was aware of the tradition on *Melita Africana* that stated that Paul not only cured Publius' father from fever and dysentery, but that he baptised him and the other islanders, and even went as far as consecrating him first bishop of Malta. Publius was reputed to have been transferred to the See of Athens where he died a martyr and saint in circa 125 A.D., having been the successor of Dionysius the Aeropagite.

Đurđević dismisses all these traditions as pious inventions. He questions the historical truth of an inscription which mentioned a certain *Prōtos Melitaíōn*.[18] The

[17] M. Buzov (2012), 500.

[18] H.C.R. Vella (1980), 27: "There is above all the testimony of a certain epigram, engraved on a big marble tomb here in Malta, with the following inscription: Λ. ΚΛ. ΥΙΟΣ. ΚΥΡ. ΙΠΠΕΥΣ ΠΩΜΑΙΩΝ, ΠΡΩΤΟΣ ΜΕΛΙΤΑΙΩΝ." In note 135 the author states: "This inscription, written, according to Abela, on one side of a spring basin and situated in the ditch beneath the former main entrance to Mdina in Malta, had been destroyed due to water-supply constructions leading to the nearby Sanatorium."

inscription or epigram on a marble slab used to be found in the ditch of Mdina and was studied by Maltese historians, like Giovanni Francesco Abela (1647), and by Quintinus (1536). This personage would have been a kind of *patronus municipii*. According to Đurđević the title of *princeps* or *primus*, given by the Vulgate is not correct, since he would have rather been a magistrate, on the type of the Greek *Archontes*, since *Melita Africana* was Hellenized when Paul was shipwrecked, and had been under Roman domination for more than 200 years.

The other two objections by Đurđević regard the fact that Publius was never bishop of *Melita Africana*, and that he could not be such in any way. Luke is silent about Publius' baptism. Moreover, according to 1Timothy 3:6, the bishop "must not be a recent convert." Thus it is impossible that the chief man of *Melítē*, Publius, was consecrated bishop within the short period of three months that Paul was supposed to have remained on the island. Đurđević also lists a number of authors and quotes martyrologies, which never mention that Publius, bishop of Athens and martyr, had ever been bishop of *Afromelita* or *Melita Africana*. He regards as fake the indication of the *Philomaltenses*, who indicate 21 January on the Martyrology as the feast of Saint Publius of Malta: *XII Kal. Febr. Athenis S. Publii Episcopi, qui Militenus a Paulo Episcopus ordinatus*. There is no link between Saint Publius, bishop of Athens and the Publius, *prōtos* of *Melita Africana*.

Chapter 7: On the Traditions of the Maltese

Đurđević dismisses many of the popular traditions of the people of *Melita Africana* as pure inventions regarding the supposed stay of Saint Paul on the island. He insists that such traditions were not so ancient as they were presented, and that many had been born out of a popular devotion encouraged by the Knights of Saint John, who were interested in finding a prestigious reason for their political power in Malta.

Among the traditions Đurđević dismisses as absurd, he mentions the supposed miracle that Paul worked when he took the venom out of all snakes in Malta, when he gave the soil and rocks of Malta miraculous healing properties, when he baptised all the inhabitants of the islands of Malta and Gozo, when he instituted troglodyte churches in the caves of the island, one of which also boasts an image of the Virgin supposedly painted by Luke, Paul's companion on the journey to Rome. Đurđević ridicules the supposition that Paul consecrated the chief man of the island, Publius, as bishop of Malta. He presents as fake miracles the preaching of the Gospel by Paul across the channel separating Malta from Gozo in order to convert the inhabitants of the sister island, and Paul's ability to strike rocks and draw a spring of pure water gushing out from the cliff face.

Đurđević is highly critical of the cult that the Maltese attribute to Saint Paul in the Grotto of Saint Paul in Rabat, outside the walls of the ancient town of *Melítē* (nowadays Mdina), where he was considered to have been "imprisoned" during his stay on the island. One of the sections of this chapter is entitled: *Vana est Traditio Maltensium de Crypta Paulina, nunc Grotta di S. Paolo*.

Another section in which Đurđević tries to discredit Maltese traditions regards the *dithálassos*, or place between two seas, in which Paul's ship was shipwrecked. The place indicated by the local tradition of *Melita Africana* is the *Cala di S. Paolo*, nowadays known as Saint Paul's Bay, at the spot where there is a cliff and a rocky islet known as Selmunett, and which Đurđević calls *insula Selmonis*. He states that the local tradition has mixed this name with another place in Crete, since Luke indicates that Paul's ship was sailing around this cape in southern Crete: *Adnavigavimus Cretae juxta Salmonem*. Thus the place in *Melita Africana* is made up and has nothing to do with the true place of the shipwreck.

An interesting note merits the section in which Đurđević dismisses as a false theory the local Maltese tradition that Paul left his collaborator Trophimus in Malta, because the latter was sick. In 2 Timothy 4:20, Paul writes: *Trophimum reliqui Mileti aegrotantem*, "I left Trophimus ill at Miletus." It is obvious that there is a confusion regarding the name of the place where Trophimus remained since Miletus is not *Melítē*. However, Đurđević is of the opinion that the reference is to *Melita Illyrica*, that is Mljet. In fact, he states: *Melitam Dalmatensem fuisse et Militenes, et Miletenes vocabulo nuncupatam*.

Chapter 8: Answers to the rest

In this last chapter Đurđević concludes his analysis by giving some answers to certain questions. The main issue concerns the voyage of Paul from *Melítē* to Rome. According to the Acts of the Apostles, after wintering on the island, Paul left *Melítē* and went to Rome by way of Syracuse, Rhegium (Reggio Calabria) and Puteoli (Pozzuoli). The ports mentioned by Luke explicitly indicate that the island from which Paul left was *Melita Africana*, namely Malta, which lies some 80 kilometres south of Sicily. Đurđević begs to differ from this theory. He states that *Melita Illyrica*, namely Mljet, was also an island where many grain ships from Alexandria would choose to winter, since it is not true that there are no safe harbours on the island. He states that there was a lot of shipping in the Adriatic between the Dalmatian coast and such ports in Italy as Ravenna, Ancona, and Brindisi. The same could be said regarding other ports in the vicinity of the Straits of Otranto, like Apollonia and Dürres (Durazzo).

The *Philomaltenses* insist that there were hardly any remains of Christian buildings on *Melita Illyrica*, whereas *Melita Africana* is full of remains of troglodyte churches from the early centuries, indicating a flourishing Christian presence on the island. But *Melita Illyrica* also has vestiges of churches going back to ancient times and the name Pavle or Pavao (Paul) is common among the islanders. The fact that the churches are destroyed is a result of the history of Mljet, which was devastated more than once by Turkish and Saracen pirates. Regarding Syracuse, Đurđević states that there were regular contacts between this important Sicilian port of *Magna Græcia* and the Adriatic coast.

A last curious but interesting section is dedicated to the *catellis Melitensium*, or the Maltese gourmet dogs, which were bred in Mljet, but which were also falsely associated with Malta. Pliny had stated that this breed of dogs was typical of Mljet in the Adriatic, but then Strabo confused the name of the island with Malta, and thus erroneously assigned this particular dog breed to the wrong island. The same thing occurred in the legend of the nymph Calypso, as we have already seen, which Đurđević associates with Mljet and not with Malta. In fact, it is associated with neither Mljet nor Gozo (Malta), but with a submerged island south of Italy, as we shall see in the next chapter.

Concluding remarks

Ignjat Đurđević's study is certainly a very erudite scholarly contribution to the centuries' old question of the place in which Saint Paul was shipwrecked on his way to Rome. He was convinced that, from ancient times, the island of Mljet in the Adriatic, known also as Meleda, or *Melita Illyrica*, was the undisputed place where the apostle of the gentiles landed in A.D. 60 on his way to Rome, after an eventful voyage that brought him to Crete and thence into the Adriatic, as a result of a strong SE gale that made his ship run aground on the southern tip of the island. According to Đurđević, this tradition, handed down since Byzantine times, encountered the fierce opposition of the Order of the Knights of Saint John, who, from 1530 to 1798, were feudal lords of the island of Malta in the centre of the Mediterranean, in what he calls the Sicilian or Libyan Sea. Malta is therefore considered to be the *Melita Africana*. Its name might sound very similar to that of Mljet, and that is why it is difficult to distinguish which is the *Melítē* of the Acts of the Apostles. Đurđević states that the Knights invented the cult of Saint Paul in Malta, and they succeeded in eradicating the same cult from the area of Dubrovnik, because of their prestige and power.

Our aim in presenting the arguments that Đurđević makes in favour of the Meleda theory has not been that of giving any credit to his reasonings, but that of being honest about his erudite preparation to write upon this argument. His knowledge of Greek and Latin, as well as that of the ancient authors of classical antiquity, particularly geographers, coupled with his love for Mljet and the Republic of Dubrovnik, were instrumental in the production of this unique volume. Indeed, Đurđević merits to be known for what he wrote, and recently his contribution has been revalued by Croatian scholars. Đurđević knew that the Maltese also had their historians and scholars, and that their theories were widely known. Indeed, many clues relating to the description that Luke gives us in the voyage diary of Acts 27-28 certainly point to Malta as the more probable place in which the apostle could have been shipwrecked. Unfortunately for the Maltese tradition, the local cult soon got mixed up with many superstitious and folkloristic imaginations that Đurđević dismisses as fake theories. His arguments are highly convincing and merit due attention.

Đurđević has the merit of having placed Mljet on the map of Paul's journeys, of which the Acts narrate three great missionary journeys and the journey to Rome. We do not know what happened later on, since there are many traditions showing Paul present in Illyria and in the Epirus region of the southern Adriatic. Maybe these traditions have been instrumental in fuelling interest on Đurđević's part in the possible location of Paul's shipwreck site on the beautiful island of Mljet.

Chapter 2

Otok Mljet and its link with the shipwreck of Saint Paul

I had the occasion to visit the Croatian island of Mljet twice, on Wednesday 29 April 2015 and on Thursday 8 June 2017.[19] My first visit was a brief one. After arriving with the car ferry at Sobra, I visited the port of Polače and the Nacionalni Park Mljet, crossing to the islet of Sveta Marija with the Benedictine monastery on the Veliko Jezero. The visit in itself was a welcome surprise to my longing to see the island which cherishes a local tradition regarding the arrival of the Apostle Paul after his shipwreck on the way to Rome. After the visit, my interest in Mljet could only increase and my desire was that of discovering the entire island, since the memories connected to Saint Paul's shipwreck were to be found in other areas of Otok Mljet. The second occasion to visit the island was therefore most welcome. This time I was much more fortunate in having one whole day to tour the island, sleeping overnight at the beach resort of Saplunara at the south-eastern tip of the island. This time I did not only visit Polače and Otočić Sveta Marija, but also other important sites related to the theory of Saint Paul's tradition on Mljet, including the twin islets of Veliki Školj and Mali Školj at Saplunara, which mark the traditional site of the shipwreck, the archaeological remains of two churches, one Byzantine and one Mediaeval, on a hill east of Korita, the cliffs above the islet Prećki Školj, which is also another traditional site for the shipwreck and, always on the southern coast of Mljet, the Odisejeva Špilja, or Odyssey Cave, a natural karst hole with a sea opening at the end. The Croatian Franciscan brother who accompanied me had already made his homework and made me get the feel of the island not only by driving me around along the roads in the various other coves and villages, like Maranovići, Okuklje, Goveđari and Pomena, but also by walking along country footpaths in the natural beauty of the pine forests of the island. This experience proved to be providential in order to contextualise the erudite study of

[19] I am grateful to Fr. Sandro Tomašević OFM, from the Franciscan Province of Zagreb, Croatia, who kindly accompanied me twice to Mljet and took the photos of this enchanting island. Had it not been for his efforts, I would never have been able to visit Mljet so thoroughly.

the Benedictine scholar and abbot Ignjat Đurđević regarding his defence of Mljet, *Melita Illyrica*, as the island where Saint Paul was shipwrecked on his way to Rome, against the theory of the *Philomaltenses*, supported by the Order of the Knights of Saint John, who defended Malta, *Melita Africana*, as the more probable location to which Acts 28:1-10 could refer.

Geography of Otok Mljet

The island of Mljet is one of the southernmost islands off the Dalmatian coast of Croatia. It lies NW of the city of Dubrovnik, facing the Pelješac peninsula, from which it is divided by the Mljetsli Kanal, and is flanked on the SE by the Elafitski Otoci, made up of Kolacep, Lopud and Šipan, 17 km northwest of Dubrovnik, Croatia, three islands which are separated from the mainland coast by the Koločepski Channel. Indeed, for any vessel coming into the Adriatic from the Straits of Otranto in a NW direction, Otok Mljet is the first large island that is met. Beyond it, on the W lies the island of Lastovo and on the NW the larger island of Korčula. Its SW coast faces the open Adriatic Sea in the direction of the Gargano Peninsula of Italy.

Mljet is a long and narrow island aligned due NW to SE. It is partly of sedimentary and partly of volcanic origin and, seen from a distance, presents a panorama of craggy crests and cliffs and deep gorges and ravines, all covered with lush Mediterranean forest. Its total length is 37 kilometres and it has an average width of 3.2 kilometres. 98 square kilometres, or a total of 84 per cent of the island, is covered with forest, dominated by the Mediterranean pine. Its climate is typically Mediterranean, with short, cool and wet winters (average temperature for January is 9° C.) and warm dry summers (average temperature for July is 24° C.). Rain is plentiful during the period October to April.

The craggy crests of the island are still untouched places of great natural beauty. The highest peak is Veliki Grad (514 metres) above Babino Polje, in the central area of the island. In the same zone are found other peaks, including Zirinje (486 metres), above the port of Sobra, Kantun (459 metres), and Katani (427 metres).

The geomorphological makeup of Mljet consists largely of limestone and dolomite rocks. The coast is characterised by craggy cliffs, with many islets and underwater rocks and shoals, but it also has some fine sheltered harbours. Indeed, Mljet was always famous as a safe haven for ships in the Adriatic. Its harbours and bays include the following, in a clockwise direction starting from Klačina Luka and Luka Sobra where the car ferry berths. Going due east is Prožurska Luka, with the islets of Galičnjak, Borovac, Veliki Školj and Senjevac. The next bay is Okuklje Bay, and then the coast proceeds to the easternmost tip of the island at Rat Vratnički.

It is at this point that the coast turns south into the small peninsula of Saplunara. This is the southernmost tip of the island. For the sake of our study, this area is particularly important because it is traditionally considered to be the exact spot of the shipwreck of Saint Paul. Indeed, there are two islets at this tip, simply called Veliki Školj and Mali Školj. They lie some metres away from the shore and are separated from it by a narrow sea channel which could be regarded as a "place between two seas" (διθάλασσον or *locus bimaris*). As I have pointed out earlier, this point of the island faces the SE, that is the open sea leading to the Straits of Otranto. It is certainly the place where a vessel could be shipwrecked in strong Jugo gale. The bay of Saplunara, facing the SW is one of the most enchanting beaches on the island.

From Saplunara the coast follows a WNW direction. It is mainly a craggy coast full of cliffs, peninsulas, gorges and islets. Of particular interest are a group of islets beyond the Dugi Rat peninsula. They include the islets of Prečki Školj, Golić, Kosmač, and Lukovac. From the high cliffs above the islets, close to the hamlet of Maranovići, one has a splendid view over the islets and it is also possible to see underwater rocks and reefs in the area. A local lady from Saplunara indicated this place as the traditional site of the shipwreck. Indeed it also faces the right direction of the Jugo gale. One should not be surprised that the site of the shipwreck is indicated in more than one spot on Mljet. The same phenomenon is evident on the island of Malta, since the exact place of Paul's shipwreck has never been determined on a satisfactory level from the scientific point of view. Local tradition, however, has its own intrinsic value which should not be underestimated.

Going further west, on the widest section of the island, and below the hamlets of Zabrežje, Sršenovići and Zadublje, which make up the main village of Babino Polje, an arduous walk down the cliff takes you to the lookout above the Odisevja Špilja, or Odysseus Cave, which is a natural karst hole in the cliff leading down to the sea below and connected to the open sea by a natural cave opening at the far end. According to Homer's *Odyssey*, after his arrival on the island of Ogygia, Odysseus spent seven years longing for his beloved Penelope, while he was held captive in love by the nymph Calypso, Atlas' daughter. There are a number of Mediterranean islands that claim to be the place where the nymph Calypso seduced Odysseus, until she was ordered by the gods to set him free. Mljet is one of them. So is the island of Gozo, where local tradition indicates a much smaller cave, which is more of cleft in the rock, overlooking the Bay of Ramla l-Ħamra, as the Cave of Calypso. This fact is another proof of the competing claims between Mljet and Malta regarding not only the shipwreck of Saint Paul but also other legends. Such claim is the result of the resemblance of the names of both islands, particularly the name *Melítē*, with which both were known. One has to admit, however, that the Odisevja Špilja on Mljet is a much more striking natural feature than the Calypso Cave of Gozo.[20]

The coast proceeds to the hamlet of Ropa, and one enters the NW section, covering one-third of the island of Mljet, which is a National Park, the Nacionalni Park Mljet. This area covers roughly the extension of the property of the Monastery of Sveta Marija, the Benedictine Monastery where abbot Ignjat Đurđević wrote his famous treatise on Mljet and the shipwreck of Saint Paul. After the two islets of Vranji Škoj and Utrnji Škoj, one finds the Solinski Kanal, the opening to the Veliko Jezero, or Great Lake. This is the lake on which the Otočić Sveta Marija stands, with the monastery and abbey church of the Benedictine monks. Originally Veliko Jezero and Malo Jezero were freshwater lakes on the northwestern section of Mljet, but the Benedictines dug a channel in order to communicate with the open sea and the lakes became sea water. We shall describe the islet of Sveta Marija in a separate section and continue on our description of Mljet. The Veliko Jezero is a paradise of deep blue and green crystal clear water, with pine trees growing right to the very edge of the shore. The pristine natural beauty of the surroundings has fortunately been left very much untouched, even though the islet of Sveta Marija is visited by many tourists who come as day trippers on Mljet.

The westernmost peninsula of the island is made up of Sparožni Rat and the tourist harbour of Pomena, another important ferry connection to the mainland. In the interior one finds the hamlet of Goveđari. Hugging the NW coast of the island are the islets of Galicja, Pomeštak, Glavat, Borovac and Maslinovac.

The principal village in the National Park of Mljet is Polače. It lies in a sheltered harbour, protected by other islets, including Moračnik, Tajnik, Ovrata and Kobrava. The name Polače evokes the Latin *Palatium*, and is known in Italian as Porto Palazzo. The bay in which the village is found is very popular with boating enthusiasts, being protected by the islets and being 5.6 kilometres long and 4 kilometres wide. The name comes from the remains of a Roman country villa dating from the 1st

[20] The exact location of Ogygia as the island of Calypso is unknown. Various Mediterranean islands claim the honour but without any historical foundation, like *Gavdos (Gaudos)*, a tiny island off the southwestern coast of Crete; Gozo in Malta, which was confused with the Cretan *Gavdos*, while its true name originally was *Gaulos* (from *Gavdos* comes the Maltese name "Għawdex" and the name Gozo given to the island); Mljet, because of the narration of Apollonius of Rhodes regarding the itinerary of Jason and the Argonauts who, in order to avoid the Bosphorus, entered the Danube River from the Black Sea and got into the Adriatic from Illyria close to the island of *Melítē* (Mljet), a story which is similar in some ways to Odysseus' journey to avoid the Straits of Messina. Apollonius, however, does not identify Ogygia with *Melítē.* He said it was farther away from the rest of the islands. For a detailed study of the probable location of Ogygia, see H.C.R. Vella (2012). According to this Maltese professor of Classics, the site of Ogygia could be Capo Colonna, close to the town of Crotone in Calabria, at the entrance to the Gulf of Taranto, quoting Pliny.

to the 6th centuries. It is one of the largest Roman buildings in Croatia after the palace of Diocletian in Split. The Roman remains are still visible, together with the remains of two Byzantine churches some distance away from the palace.[21]

The coast looking towards the Pelješac peninsula on the mainland leads you back to Sobra, from where our geographical description of the island of Mlejt started.

Brief History of Otok Mljet

Mljet was first discovered by the ancient Greek and Roman cartographers. The name of island in classical antiquity was *Melítē*. The Romans conquered it in 167 B.C. and called it *Melita*. It was also known by other names, including *Meleta, Malta, Meleda*, especially from Mediæval times. The descriptions of the island by Greek and Roman geographers are examined by Đurđević in his study. The inhabitants of the island were Serbian pirates from the Neretva region and the island of Korčula. They were described in the 10th century by Emperor Constantine Porphyrogenitus, in *De Administrando Imperio*. He called the region of Mljet and the lower Neretva by the name Pagania, since the tribes that inhabited these regions accepted Christianity only about 890, some 250 years later than other Slavs. They were known as Pagani or Narentani. In ancient times, they were expert pirates who attacked shipping from Alexandria to Aquileia. That is why the Emperor Augustus had to subdue them in 35 B.C. They continued to practice piracy also against the Venetians, until they were crushed by the Doge Pietro Orseolo II in 998.

When the Romans occupied Mljet, they called it *Melita*, a name meaning "Island of Honey." However, this name was used also for the island of Malta in the Mediterranean. Mljet became an important Roman colony, and was famous for the production of wine, olive oil and honey.

According to Apollonius of Rhodes, *Agronautica*, IV,4, "Μελίτη gave her name to a mountain on the island (of Korčula) and was also the name of an island to the north, modern Mljet off the Croatian coast."[22]

---

21 T. Turković (2011). The original thesis about this palace was that it was constructed by Agesilaus from Anasarba in Cilicia, who was exiled to the island of Mljet by Emperor Septimius Severus (145-211 AD). The ruins of this palace, however, were probably built as an extravagant villa (according to some a hunting lodge) by Pierius in 498 A.D., to whom Odoacer, king of Italy, has given Mljet in settlement of a debt. See Z. Springer, www.croatianhistory.net (accessed 18 June 2017).

22 Apollonius Of Rhodes (2015), 155.

We have already referred in chapter 1 to the discussion regarding the name *Melítē* in Strabo and Ptolemy. In Pliny the Elder, the reference to the name *Melita* is certainly that of Mljet in the Adriatic.[23]

The reference to Mljet by the Byzantine Emperor Constantine VII Porphyrogenitus in his *De Administrando Imperio* (c. 950) was fundamental in the subsequent development of the island's history. Not only did it provide the foundation of the thesis regarding Saint Paul's shipwreck on the island, but it further consolidated the Christian tradition on Mljet. When the emperor wrote his treatise, he mentioned the inhabitants of *Meleta* and the nearby islands by the name of Narentines or Pagani, and states that they were unbaptised:

> "In Pagania are the inhabited cities of Mokron, Beroullia, Ostrok and Slavinetza. Also, they possess these islands: the larger island of Kourkra (Korčula), or Kiker, on which there is a city; another large island, Meleta, or Malozeatai, which St. Luke mentions in the Acts of the Apostles by the name of Melítē, in which a viper fastened upon Saint Paul by his finger, and Saint Paul burnt it up in the fire; another large island, Phara (Hvar); another large island, Bratzis (Brač). There are other islands not in possession of these same Pagani: the island of Choara, the island of Ies, the island of Lastobon (Lastovo)."[24]

In 1151 Otok Mljet became linked with the presence of the Benedictine monks who crossed the Adriatic from Pulsano on the Gulf of Taranto in Apulia and from Monte Gargano. The monks came ashore at Sutmiholjska cove. They became the feudal lords of the island and built the beautiful monastery of Sveta Marija on the tiny island on Veliko Jezero. The church was built in 1187 by the Serbian prince Desa of the House of Vojislavljević. It was consecrated in 1198, according to a document published by Pope Innocent III. Although the church was built in a Romanesque style, which is still evident in the interior, it eventually also assumed Renaissance and Baroque features. The Benedictines renounced the property of the entire island in 1345, and eventually only kept the northern one-third area of Otok Mljet, in the same area now occupied by the National Park. In 1410, the island became property of the Republic of Dubrovnik, but in a contract stipulated with the Benedictines, it was agreed that the Municipality of Babino Polje had to pay an annual compensation to the monks. Adjacent to the abbey church, a monastery was built in Renaissance style, with a cloister having arches on one side and a strong fortified tower to defend the edifice. During the 16th century, this became an important monastery, and was the headquarters of the Benedictine *Congregatio Melitensis*, which included all the Benedictine monasteries present in the Republic of Dubrovnik. It was in this monastery that lived two famous Benedictine monks who were erudite poets and writers, namely abbot Mavro Vetranović Kavčić and abbot Ignjat Đurđević. By the end of the 18th century, the Benedictines had left

---

[23] H.C.R. Vella (1995), 11-13.

[24] Constantine Porphyrogenitus, *De Administrando Imperio,* 36.

Mljet and retreated to the Monastery of Sveti Jakov outside Dubrovnik. In 1809, during the rule of Napoleon, the Mljet monastery was disbanded. When Austria took over the island, it placed the forestry office in the building. As we have already seen, between the world wars, the building was owned by the Ragusa (Dubrovnik) Bishopric. In 1960 it became a hotel, and in 1998 it was returned to the diocese of Dubrovnik. At present, it is being restored to its former splendour.

The monastery of Sveta Marija on Veliko Jezero

The tiny round island of Sveta Marija lies in the Nacionalni Park Mljet and is accessible to visitors who are on visit to the National Park and take the short boat ride to the island. The entire island is occupied by the monastery, above which rises a small hill providing splendid views over Veliko Jezero, surrounded by lush greenery and pine trees. The church of Sveta Marija is the central point of attraction on the island. It is a rather small church, built in Romanesque style with further Renaissance and Baroque additions. It has a plan of a Latin cross, with three altars and a dome. The main altar is dedicated to the Virgin Mary. It is a typical Benedictine altar with a cross in the front and stands in an apse having a stained-glass window of the Assumption of the Blessed Virgin. The side altars also stand in apses and have paintings encased in baroque marble frames. One of the paintings depicts Saint Benedict, founder of the Benedictines. The church has a porch from which one enters into the main building. Inside there are some ancient tomb slabs, commemorating important burials. Together with other visitors, here came the son of King Toma of Bosnia, who died in this place and was buried in the sanctuary of the Virgin. A good description of the monastery with maps and plans is found in a paper by Josip Stošić:

> "In the Mljet National Park there are two world monuments of architecture. The 5th century palace in the Polače Cove and, on the small island in the centre of the Lake, the church dating back to the late 12th century with the monastery which has been in the present form since the 16th century. This church, consecrated to St. Mary, is a remarkable structure, the best-proportioned and most complete among the group of single-nave buildings with a dome in a square body, within which it figures prominently by the size of its dome and its three-part shrine. In the 13th century, a bell tower was built next to the church, which was later replaced with a vestibule partially raised in three levels. A defence tower was built above the vestibule in the Renaissance, and in front of it is the Renaissance cloister from which one enters the church and the monastery. Along the church complex extends the High Renaissance 16th century monastery with three open levels. The lower level is open with arcades towards the sea, the central with a cloister towards the courtyard, and the top level has a terrace facing the sea along the entire front. Thus, the monastery looked like a villa until the second half of the 16th century when, due to the increased danger of pirates, they turned it into a fort by adding the tower."[25]

---

[25] J. Stošić (1998), 7-21.

The tradition of the shipwreck of Saint Paul on Mljet

One of the most important reasons to go to Mljet is that of visiting one of the possible places where Saint Paul was shipwrecked on his way from Caesarea to Rome in A.D. 60. Maybe few people are aware of the ancient tradition present on Mljet regarding the presence of Paul of Tarsus, since the popular belief, corroborated also by scholarly analysis and biblical exegesis, points to the Mediterranean island of Malta as the true place of the shipwreck. As we have already stated, the tradition of the shipwreck of the Apostle on Mljet goes back to the Byzantine Emperor Constantine VII Porphyrogenitus, author of *De Administrando Imperio* (948 – 952). He states that the island of *Melítē* in the Adriatic was the place where Paul was bitten by a viper, which he then threw into the fire and suffered no harm, according to Acts of the Apostles 28:1-10. The name of the island, *Melítē*, as we have seen, is attributed to both Mljet and Malta, and this is the reason for the double tradition of the shipwreck of the Apostle.

It is not our aim at this point to defend the truthfulness of the opinion of the majority of scholars, namely that Malta is the true island of the shipwreck. What we intend to do is to delve into the local traditions of Mljet in order to examine how the thesis of Paul's shipwreck on the island came about and was so staunchly defended by Ignjat Đurđević in 1730. We shall do so on the basis of our personal visit to Mljet and the contact with the places that take pride in being considered as possible locations for the presence of Saint Paul on this Dalmatian island.

The exact location of the shipwreck of the Apostle on Mljet is not known. But then, neither is it known with exactitude in Malta itself. The whole problem hinges on the Greek word διθάλασσον, translated into Latin as *locus bimaris*, or "a place between two seas." In other words, the place of the shipwreck could have been preferably a shoal (since the vessel ran aground according to Acts) or maybe an undersea rock. The word *dithálassos* can also mean a promontory, washed by the sea on both sides. In both Malta and Mljet sandbars and shoals are rare, since both islands are extremely rocky and full of craggy cliffs. That is why, in both cases, the place of the shipwreck is traditionally linked with an islet which is close enough to the shore, from which it is separated by a sea channel, thus being "a place between two seas", namely an outer sea and an inner sea. In Malta the traditional place (by no means proven to be the actual spot) is indicated in the islet of Selmunett, or as it is known, Saint Paul's Island, at the entrance to Saint Paul's Bay. In the case of Mljet the site of the shipwreck is traditionally placed at the extreme southeastern section of the island, close to the tourist resort and beach of Saplunara. Indeed, at this point, there are two islets, known by the names Veliki Školj and Mali Školj. They are tiny islets some metres away from the shore of Saplunara, forming an inner sea channel and facing the open sea on their outer sides. These islets look towards the E and SE. Given that, in the Adriatic, the SE gale, known as Jugo, blows directly towards this coast of Mljet, and given also that the sea currents on the Dalmatian coast of the Adriatic run in a SE to NW direction, that is, hugging the coast itself, a vessel that was caught in a Jugo gale would have followed the coast upwards from the Straits of Otranto, and would have headed directly towards Mljet and to this particular section of the coast.[26]

The meteorological analysis of the Jugo wind is correct in the case of the Adriatic, but obviously raises many questions. If Paul's ship was caught in a gale off the coast of Crete, some kilometres in the open sea from Cape Matala and passed under the lee of Cauda (*Gavdos*), the direction of the gale was ENE. In order to drive the ship into the Straits of Otranto and into the Adriatic, the direction of the gale must have changed at a certain point, and from an ENE gale it veered to a SSE gale, namely, the Jugo. How this meteorological phenomenon could have occurred is anybody's guess. What we do know is that the ENE gale could have carried the ship towards the Syrtis Banks in Libya and somehow it carried it further to the north, towards Malta. The SSE gale, at whatever point it found the ship in the Ionian Sea, would have carried it due north towards Cephalonia and into the Straits of Otranto and on to Mljet. What is difficult to comprehend is where exactly did the Jugo gale originate. Maybe a detailed meteorological study of the origins of the Jugo wind in the Adriatic can provide some clues for defending the Mljet theory of Saint Paul's shipwreck.

---

[26] M. Buzov (2012), 500-501: "Based on the analyis of hydrometeorological elements of the southeast coast of the island of Mljet and the maritime features of ancient ships, the records from the Acts of the Apostles as well as considerations and interpretations of various authors, Miloš Brajević and Stjepo Đurđević-Tomaš put forward the idea that St. Paul's shipwreck took place on the southeastern coast of Mljet in a bay with a straight shoreline. The authors' interpretation of the term 'bay with a straight shoreline,' from the Acts of the Apostles denotes a bay offering the possibility of a safe disembarkment or where the castaways could safely land ashore. However, while approaching the 'bay with a straight shoreline' the ship hit an underwater rock. Neverthless, even though there must have also been non-swimmers among the castaways, everyone was saved, indicating that the shore was near and most likely sheltered from the rough seas. The Uvala Nad Garma and Uvala Podškolj bays, with the islets of Veliki Školj and Mali Školj, offer excellent shelter from the southeastern wind and waves, allowing safe landing to the castaways. In the opinion of Brajević and Đurđević-Tomaš, the bay of Veliki Školj and Mali Školj matches the description of *Dithalassos* by Saint Luke, i.e., a place open to two seas. From the sailing experience of the authors, when a sailor looks from a ship a cable's length from Veliki Školj during the southeastern wind, he has the illusion that there are indeed two seas; a stormy sea hitting the rock on the southeastern side, and a quiet sea on the northwest side, providing safe shelter. The described locations according to Đurđević, Plankoi and Ničetić match all maritime descriptions, and especially the visual descriptions from the Acts of the Apostles, proving it possible that St. Paul may have been shipwrecked on the southeast coast of Mljet, in a 'bay with a straight shoreline.' The authors consider the opinion of Palunko and Ničetić plausible, based on the depth and position of Veliki Školj and Mali Školj, which form a natural breakwater, that is, a 'double sea'."

The Acts of the Apostles speak about the natives of *Melítē* as being hospitable and having welcomed the shipwrecked prisoners and crew with rare kindness. They are described as οἵ τε βάρβαροι, or "barbarians", an expression which is normally taken to refer to persons who could not speak Greek. We have already noted, however, that there are other meanings that this expression could have, particularly the meaning of peasants or farmers, derived from the oriental word *barr*. According to Đurđević the inhabitants of *Melita Africana* could not possibly have been "barbarians" since their language was Punic, but Greek was also commonly known on the island, whereas the inhabitants of *Melita Illyrica* were primitive tribes who could not speak any classical language. Maybe the most important thing about these natives was that they were all simple folk, that is, peasants and farmers, and that is why they are called "barbarians", whether they inhabited Malta or Mljet. What is typically true of Mljet is what Đurđević states regarding the local inhabitants, when he states that they are *incolae simplices ac rudes, sed perquam hospitales*, "simple and rustic inhabitants, but very hospitable." The island is still inhabited by locals, many of whom are nowadays employed in the flourishing tourist industry of the island. When touring the island's hamlets, the Croatian Franciscan brother who accompanied me took me to a hamlet called Prožura. There was a group of elderly persons sitting in the shade, and the impression they gave was that of simple and hospitable country folk. Even the young lady who gave us the information we needed to enter the National Park, and who came from this same hamlet, showed a great sense of kindness and charm in dedicating her time to our questions. The same attitude was present in the small supermarket at Polače, where we asked for a packed lunch during our visit to the various sights of the island. The lady who owned our holiday apartment was also very kind in indicating the local tradition of Saint Paul present in another location linked with the shipwreck, close to the islets of Prečki Školj, Golić, Kosmač, and Lukovac, where one sees underwater reefs.

The remains of the two churches near Korita are of particular interest. From the road leading from Korita to Saplunara a narrow country lane branches off to the right, and after about 800 metres one arrives at the remains of two superimposed churches. "Recent archaeological investigations on Mljet, yielded the remains of another early Christian basilica, which – according to the tradition – might belong to a church of Saint Paul, as well as yet another one that could be dated to the end of the 11th century. The basilica occupies the southeast part of the island, near the Veli Školj islet, the place where we believe Saint Paul's ship ran aground, as documented by Vicko Palunko. The former church can be dated to the 5th/6th century. The remains of the churches confirm the existence of a significant Christian community on Mljet."[27]

---

[27] M. Buzov (2009), 501.

The two churches are totally in ruins, and only the foundation stones are visible nowadays. The first church is the larger one. This is a Byzantine basilica with a double aisle and an apse. It is dated 5th to 6th century and is thus a proof that Mljet was already Christianised by this time. The second church is the smaller one within the large Basilica. It is also made up of a single aisle with three apses and is of mediaeval origin, probably dating to the 11th/12th centuries. The masonry of the churches indicates that the stones originated from Roman *villae* (country villas) which are common on the Dalmatian coast, particularly in the region of Zadar. The same island of Mljet has a *villa* in the palace of Polače where we have noted that there are the remains of another two churches.

The fact that these two churches are found close to Korita and not far from Saplunara indicates that they were, in a sense, linked with the cult of the shipwreck of Saint Paul on Mljet. Obviously, this is not a proof of the truthfulness of the tradition, but it is a good indication. The same thing can be found in Malta, where the traditional place of the shipwreck is also marked by a small mediaeval church built on the opposite coast of Saint Paul's Bay, which is mentioned by Jean Quintinus in 1536, and is locally known as *San Pawl tal-Ħġejjeġ* (Saint Paul of the bonfires). The church lies close to a rocky promontory some distance away from *Il-Blat tal-Għażżenin*, where there are underwater reefs and craggy rocks. This promontory was believed to mark the exact spot of the shipwreck.[28] On Mljet these two churches lie on a hill in full view of Saplunara Bay, and they might have been built to honour the sacred tradition of the shipwreck of the Apostle in this section of Otok Mljet.

An interesting study on the probability that Saint Paul was shipwrecked on Mljet is provided in a study in Croatian by Antun Ničetić, summarised in the following Abstract in English:

> "The author examines Saint Paul's journey from Caesarea to Rome as described by Saint Luke in the Acts of the Apostles, chapters 27 and 28. The voyage to Rome did not develop according to the plan due to the strong northeast wind which blew the ship off the course and away from the coast of Crete. After fourteen days of wandering, the ship was wrecked on the island of *Melita*. The Acts of the Apostles, being primarily a religious source, produces insufficient navigational, meteorological, oceanographic or other affiliated data which could aid an accurate reconstruction of Saint Paul's travel from Crete to *Melita*, and farther west to Puteoli. It is generally believed that this incident took place on Malta, the island at the time known as *Melita*. Equally so, *Melita* could have been the island of Mljet in the southern Adriatic since the latter was referred to under the same name at the time. Having

[28] In the *Cala di San Paolo* of Malta, the shallow promontory, where *Il-Gillieru* restaurant stands, divides what used to be one beach, the western side being taken over by a small harbour. This, according to Quintinus, was the site (*ibi devotissimus*) and not the rocks known as *Il-Blat tal-Għażżenin*. Quintinus' statement gains credence because he himself did not believe it, but was simply reporting what the Maltese told him. I thank Professor Vella for drawing my attention to this important detail.

analysed the Acts and the sources adverted to in this article, the author's aim is to discuss the navigational, meteorological, oceanographic and other natural conditions which could have carried Saint Paul's ship to the shores of Mljet. Considerable evidence, however, does suggest that it was more likely for the wind and currents to drift him to the southeast coast of Mljet rather than the northeast coast of Malta, and the site today known as Saint Paul's Bay. Here are the author's arguments in support of the aforementioned thesis: Saint Paul's ship was unable to sail close to the wind nor take advantage of a beam wind and, therefore, could not have sailed in the northeast wind with the course due west from Crete to the northwest coast of Malta. The use of the sea anchor contributes to the speculation that Paul's ship was running before the wind, and could not have, therefore, sailed from Crete to Malta in the northeast wind, whilst the southeast wind could only have brought him to the coast of Mljet. Saint Luke's records of «sailing to and fro across Adria» undoubtedly refer to the change of the wind course. In all likelihood, the direction of the wind did change, and northeast wind did not blow the entire fortnight, as generally stated in literature. Had the northeast wind blown throughout those fourteen days, Saint Paul's ship would have been wrecked off the shores of northern Africa. However, that was not the case, for it appears that the vessel was carried by southeast winds, Scirocco most likely, the prevailing wind in this part of the Ionian and Adriatic Sea during the months Saint Paul's voyage took place. Owing to these winds, the ship managed to avoid a shipwreck in the Gulf of Sidra, but drifted off its course to Mljet. The south wind could not have brought St. Paul's ship to the north-western (sic!) coast of Malta. Currents of the eastern Mediterranean, Ionian, and Adriatic Sea flow anticlockwise, and therefore headed the ship towards Mljet, and away from Malta. Regular route of merchant ships carrying wheat from Alexandria to Puteoli, that is, Rome, followed the eastbound tracks along the coastline and islands of the eastern Mediterranean and Ionian Sea, passing through the Strait of Otranto, and farther along the coastline of southern Italy, by the Strait of Messina to Puteoli and Rome. It all leads to the conclusion that the Alexandrian ship may well have reached Mljet (and not Malta), picked up Saint Paul and the shipwreck survivors, who had remained on the island for three months, and set off for Puteoli. From the abovementioned account of Saint Luke one may conclude that Saint Paul's ship was in the Adriatic (and not only in the Ionian Sea as references state) for, after a fortnight's voyage, Saint Paul reached an unknown island, later to learn of its name - *Melita*. Beyond doubt, *Melita* must have been the island of Mljet. Nature has equipped Mljet with inlets and bays which had provided shelter from all the winds and stormy seas to the seafarers of antiquity and later periods. This is quite contrary to the statements of some authors according to which Mljet offers no safe harbours. Most recent archaeological excavations have pointed to the existence of an additional Early Christian basilica which is said to have belonged to the Church of Saint Paul. The building is located on the south-eastern part of the island, in the very vicinity of the islet of Veli Školj (Cima di Meleda), where V. Palunko believed Saint Paul's vessel suffered a shipwreck. Christianity gained a strong foothold on Mljet as indicated by the remains of two sixth-century basilicas in Polače, and other archaeological findings bearing Christian symbols of Syrian and Palestinian origin, dating from the 5th and 6th centuries. As the Byzantine emperor Constantine VII Porphyrogenitus recorded in his writings, Saint Paul, having been bitten in the arm by a snake on the island of Mljet, threw the snake into the fire. According to the author, it is plausible that the wind and the currents headed Saint Paul's ship to the shore of the island of Mljet."[29]

[29] A. Ničetić (2000), 305-370. We quote the Abstract in English at the end of the paper.

The question of Saint Paul's shipwreck on Mljet. An unresolved question

The experience I gained upon visiting twice Otok Mljet in order to see for myself the places associated with Saint Paul's shipwreck convinced me that the theories of Ignjat Đurđević are not to be taken lightly. Coming from the island of Malta, which boasts the honour of having welcomed Paul in A.D. 60 when he was shipwrecked on its shores on his way to Rome, I am obviously inclined to dismiss the Mljet theory as highly improbable. Before even coming to Mljet I had refused it *a priori* as a pure invention. I remain convinced that the meteorological data we possess nowadays are convincing in pointing to the fact that the gale that carried Paul's ship away from Crete in the direction of the Syrtis Banks in North Africa ended up by directing the ship on a more northerly course in an ENE direction towards Malta. At least this is what convinces me every time I experience the *Gregale* gale, locally known as *Grigal* in Malta, which is a humid gale-force wind (could reach force 8 and beyond), blowing from Mount Ida in Crete towards Malta, especially during the months of November and December. My observations of the pounding waves on the northeast coast of Malta make me believe that Paul ended up on this island and not in the Adriatic.

Having said this, however, I cannot remain silent about my surprise in discovering that the tradition of Saint Paul on Mljet is by no means an invention. If one is after the exact spot where Paul was shipwrecked, he is bound to end up disappointed both on Mlejt and on Malta. Whatever theories have been brought forward in Malta to determine the exact location of the shipwreck, none is convincing. We have to rely on local tradition. The same can be said of Mljet. I am not convinced that the site of Saplunara is definitely the place of the shipwreck, for various reasons. First, because the site is not a sand bar but a rocky islet. Second, because it faces the southeast, and although it would be the perfect spot for a shipwreck during a Jugo gale, one needs to have a lot of imagination to figure out how a ship running under the lee of *Gavdos* in the direction of the Syrtis Banks could possibly have found its way northwards into the Straits of Otranto and into the Adriatic, and on to Mljet. True, sea currents in the Adriatic follow the Illyrian coast northwards, but the sudden radical change in the wind direction is hard to imagine.

Mljet remains much of a paradise. It is true that visitors who fall in love with this enchanting island want to return. I experienced this sensation myself. Maybe because Mljet is still untouched by savage development. Maybe because of its charm and mysterious allurement reminiscent of Odysseus' legendary seven-year stay trapped in the love-net woven for him by Calypso. What goes beyond mere fantasy and emotion is, however, more important. Mljet is an island which hides secrets of a fruitful Christian presence since Byzantine times. The remains of churches are proof of this. And then Mljet is blessed to have been the property of the Benedictine monastic Order for some 700 years. The decription that abbot Đurđević gives in his study on Saint Paul and Mljet is truly a clear photograph of the true face of Mljet. The National Park which houses the islet of Sveta Marija with the Benedictine monastery is truly a paradise, in which the deep blue hues of the water and sky embrace the lush greenery of the Mediterranean pine forests all around on the surrounding hills and peninsulas.

If Saint Paul truly stayed on Mljet is still a question which is unresolved. His intention to go to Illyricum is expressed particularly in his plan to leave Titus in charge of the church in these regions. It could very well be that Paul did visit Mljet and Illyricum after his first captivity in Rome. This would explain the cult of Saint Paul on Mljet and even in the Republic of Dubrovnik. In Romans 15:19, Paul writes: "So from Jerusalem all the way to Illyricum, I have fully proclaimed the Gospel of Christ."

According to the Pastoral Letters, after the two year captivity in Rome was over, Paul would have followed this itinerary. He would first have gone to Spain (Rom 15:24), as Clement of Rome also states. Then he went to Ephesus together with Timothy, and resided for a brief time in Macedonia after leaving Timothy in Ephesus (1Tim 1:3). From there he crossed over to Crete, where he left Titus in charge of the church on the island (Tit 1:5). Paul then visited Nicopolis in Epirus (Tit 3:12).[30] This is the moment when he would have set foot on Illyricum. Nicopolis is found at Preveza in Greece, to the north of Cephalonia in the direction of the island of Corfù. That means that it would have been easy for Paul to sail into the Adriatic and visit the coast of Illyricum, including Mljet.

Concluding remarks

Remaining on the level of reasonable conjecture, we can conclude that there exists a probability that Paul did, in fact, visit the island of Mljet in his apostolic journeys. Whether he did so as a castaway during his epic journey to Rome, or else later on, after he was freed from the first Roman captivity, is a question open to debate. What is important is that the cult of Saint Paul on Mljet does have ancient origins and is a sign of a long tradition that has linked this enchanting Dalmatian island of *Melita Illyrica* with the Apostle of the Gentiles, just as occurred in the other Mediterranean island of *Melita Africana* which boasts pride of place in being an apostolic church founded by Paul of Tarsus during the three months he spent marooned on the island before proceeding for Rome.

---

30 A.M. Buscemi (1997), 257-258.

Chapter 3

Giovanni Antonio Ciantar, *De Beato Paulo Apostolo in Melitam*

The publication of Ignjat Đurđević's study on Saint Paul's shipwreck on the island of Mljet was received with great interest, but also with apprehension, by erudite Maltese scholars, particularly those linked with the rule of the Order of the Knights of Saint John. During the 18th century, Malta was seen as a bulwark of Catholicism against the threat of the Turkish empire. Its history during the preceding two centuries had been intimately linked with this crusading spirit of the Knights. The Order had arrived in Malta in 1530, after having been ousted from Rhodes by Suleiman the Magnificent in 1522, and after having had to reluctantly accept the arid islands of Malta and Gozo, plus the garrison of Tripoli, as a fief from Emperor Charles V. Although the Knights settled in Malta with difficulty during the first years of their stay, they soon had to face the onslaught of Suleiman, who sent an armada in May 1565 to beseige the islands, after he furiously saw how the Knights plundered his vessels in the Mediterranean, contrary to their promise when they had left Rhodes. The Great Siege of Malta, which was lifted on 7 September 1565, was seen as a victorious triumph for the Order against the might of the Ottoman Turks. The participation of the Knights during the Battle of Lepanto in 1570 further enhanced the prestige of the Order. For the next two centuries the Order of Saint John was to make of Malta the southernmost bulwark of Catholic Europe against Islam.

The Knights not only brought with them their European and Christian traditions, they saw to it that the Maltese would become obedient subjects and fervent Catholics. They gave to the Maltese islands their typical Catholic character, which is still evident externally in the many magnificent baroque churches in the various *casali* or villages, which until a few decades ago dominated the Maltese skyline. The Knights knew that Malta could be seen as an important and strategic island not only for defence purposes, but also for the propagation of the Catholic faith. The fact that local tradition had long held that Saint Paul himself had been shipwrecked on the island and evangelised the Maltese inhabitants to embrace the Christian faith became, for the Knights, the *raison d'être* for their style of monastic and military rule on the islands.

It was particularly during the Grandmastership of Alof de Wignacourt (1601-1622) that the cult of Saint Paul took a strong foothold in Malta. It had been present ever since mediaeval times, and no doubt even before, since the island abounded with evidence of places of cult in troglodyte churches and some Byzantine remains.[31] The centre for the Pauline cult in Malta was established in the Grotto of Saint Paul outside the walls of the town of Notabile, in Rabat, an area under which are spread various Christian catacombs, known as the Catacombs of Saint Paul, the Catacombs of Saint Catald and the Catacombs of Saint Agatha. It was at this place, which had been venerated at least since 1336 when an *ecclesia Sancti Pauli de crypta* is mentioned, that a church dedicated to Saint Publius, who had welcomed Paul to Malta, was built by Knight-hermit Juan Benegas de Cordoba. Later on, in 1692, a large collegiate church was erected adjacent to the Grotto, namely the church of Saint Paul, the work of architect Lorenzo Gafà, which was built by funds donated by the noble lady Guzmana Navarra. Since 1610, during the time of Grand Master Wignacourt, Pope Paul V instituted a college of Canons in the Grotto, with a college for conventual chaplains and a Chapter hall close by.[32] It was also Wignacourt who took care to rebuild the medieval church of *San Paolo al mare*, which replaced a more ancient church. The church, built in 1617, marked the spot where Paul and his companions were welcomed ashore after the shipwreck in this bay.

These events were instrumental in enhancing the cult of Saint Paul on the island of Malta, during the times of the Knights of Saint John. When Đurđević wrote his treatise in 1730, he was aware of the importance of this cult of Saint Paul in Malta, and he himself was well informed regarding the sites linked with the presence of the apostle on the island. It was to be expected that his thesis regarding Mljet as the possible island where Paul was shipwrecked in the Adriatic, would have enkindled an apologetic response on the part of Maltese historians and on the part of the Order of Saint John.

This response was entrusted to a famous Maltese historian and scholar, namely Giovanni Antonio Ciantar, who published a parallel treatise to that of Đurđević eight years after the Benedictine Abbot had published his volume in 1730. In 1738, Ciantar published in Venice the volume *De Beato Paulo Apostolo in Melitam*,[33] defending the thesis in favour of Paul's shipwreck on the island of Malta.

---

[31] M. Buhagiar (2002), 253-283; M. Borg (2014).

[32] J. Azzopardi (ed.) (1990).

[33] G.A. Ciantar, *De B. Paulo Apostolo in Melitam Siculo Adriatici Maris Insulam Naufragio ejecto dissertationes apologeticae*. In inspectiones anticriticas R.P.D. Ignatii Georgii de Melitensi Apostoli Naufragio, descripto in Act. Apost. Cap. XXVII & XXVIII, auctore C. Jo. Antonio Ciantar, quae autem in praesenti opere continetur, pagina post Praefationem docebit, Venetiis, apud Christophorum Zane, Superiorum Facultatae ac Privilegio, MDCCXXXVIII.

Biography of Giovanni Antonio Ciantar[34]

Giovanni Antonio Ciantar was born in Valletta on 4 September 1696, the son of a noble family which had settled in Malta during the 15th century. When he was fifteen years old, in October 1711, he journeyed to Maiorca, Genoa, Pisa, Florence, Siena and Livorno. He then settled in Rome, where he studied at the Collegio Nazareno, dedicating himself to the study of law and literature, under the direction of Padre Paolo Chelucci. He next studied theology under Padre Benedetto Cellesi. Besides Rome, he also stayed in various Italian cities, among which Naples and Palermo, where he arrived in 1721. He was also offered prestigious posts by the viceroy of Sicily, but he returned to Rome, and in 1723 was again in Malta. Back home he married Teodora, daughter of Count Ignazio Wizzini Paleologo, and became father of a numerous family. Some of his children died when they were still young. He became one of the four Jurats or administrators of Malta. Because of his formation in literature, he became a member of the *Accademia degli Intronati* di Siena and of the Colombaria of Florence. In 1745, King Louis XV endowed him with the honour of being member of the *Academie Royale des Inscriptions et Belles Lettres de la Ville de Paris*. When he was 55, he lost his eyesight, but continued to dictate and publish various works, thanks to his good memory and erudition. He possessed a fine library and a museum in his own house. He was also a scholar of antiquities, particularly having the ability to interpret ancient insciptions found in Malta. Giovanni Antonio Ciantar died on 14 November 1778.

Ciantar was a prolific writer of Latin and Italian. The island of Malta, which was a feudal dependency of the crown of Sicily, under the leadership of the Order of the Knights of Saint John (1530-1798), lived within the sphere of the Italian cultural influence. In 1592, in the new city of Valletta, a Jesuit College was founded, on the model of the Collegio Romano. In 1769, this College became the University of Malta. In 1642, the first printing press was introduced on the island, and thus local publications appeared more frequently. One of the first among these works was that of Giovanni Francesco Abela, *Della descrittione di Malta*, published in 1647. Unfortunately, the continual struggle between the Order, the local bishop and the papal inquisitor led to many suspicions regarding publications, and it was not before 1756 that the whole question of censorship was resolved between the authorities, and the printing press of the Order could resume its activity. This is the reason why many of the works of Ciantar were published in Italy, although some manuscripts survive in the National Library of Valletta.

---

[34] G. Mangion (1981).

Ciantar published a book of Latin epigrams, entitled *Epigrammaton Libri III*, Romae 1722. Next he published the volume *De B. Paulo Apostolo in Melitam Siculo-Adriatici Maris Insulam Naufragio Eiecto disserationes apologeticae*, Venetiis 1738, which is the polemic work against the thesis of the Benedictine Abbot Ignjat Đurđević, who defended the position that Saint Paul was not shipwrecked in Malta (*Melita Africana*), but in Mljet (*Melita Illyrica)*, or Meleda, in the Adriatric.

One of Ciantar's contemporaries was Giovanni Pietro Francesco Agius De Soldanis (1712-1770), author of *Discours apologétique contre la dissertation historique et critique sur le naufrage de St. Paul dans la Mer Adriatique, pubbliée par Mr. l'Abbé Ladvocat, bibliothecaire de la Sorbonne*, Avignon 1757, with an Italian edition published in Venice in 1758. Ciantar's defence of the Maltese position was also published in a volume entitled *Critica dei critici moderni, che dall'anno 1730 infino al 1760 scrissero sulla controversia del naufragio di s. Paolo apostolo, descritto nei Capi 27 e 28 degli Atti apostolici*, Venezia 1763.

The most important of Ciantar's works was his new edition of the history of Malta by Giovanni Francesco Abela (1582-1665): *Malta illustrata ovvero descrizione di Malta isola del Mare Siciliano e Adriatico, con le sue antichità ed altre notizie, divisa in quattro libri, del commendatore fra Giovanfrancesco Abela, vicecancelliere della Sagra ed Eminentissima Religione Gerosolimitana, corretta, accresciuta e continovata dal conte Giovannantonio Ciantar*. This voluminous work in two volumes *in folio*, with a total of 1415 pages, was published in Malta in 1772 (books 1 and 2) and in 1780 (books 3 and 4), when Ciantar had already died. The volumes were dedicated respectively to Grand Masters Emmanuel De Rohan-Polduc and Manoel Pinto de Fonseca.

Introductory Contents of *De Beato Paulo Apostolo in Melitam*

Ciantar's 470 page volume is an effort to respond to the thesis of the *Philodalmatae*, who defended the island of Mljet as the place where Paul was shipwrecked on his journey to Rome. Just as Đurđević was the leader of the *Philodalmatae* with his erudite publication of 1730, Ciantar became the spokesman for the *Philomaltenses* with this volume, published in 1738, which is structured according to the same pattern of that of the Croatian Benedictine Abbot.

The volume begins with a dedication to Maria Anna Josepha of Austria, Queen consort of Portugal (1683-1754) dated 2 November 1737. This is followed by a preface and by the approval of the inquisitors in Padua, the same authorities who had declared Đurđević's work as being free of doctrinal errors.

The first section of the volume is entitled *Melitae descriptio*. It is a long description of the island of Malta and its dependencies, taking into consideration its geography and rich historical tradition. The description given by Ciantar was to provide the material that went into a much more detailed publication by the same Ciantar, which was published in two volumes, but which was the final version of a work by another famous Maltese historian, namely Count Giovanni Francesco Abela (1582-1655).[35] The work is entitled *Malta Illustrata, ovvero descrizione di Malta, isola del Mare Siciliano e Adriatico, con le sue antichità e altre notizie, divisa in quattro Libri.*

In the description of Malta, Ciantar attaches great importance to the memories of the presence of Saint Paul on the island. He mentions the *Cala di San Paolo*, or Saint Paul's Bay, and the *locum dithalassum, ac praedia Principis insulae nomine Publii*, a clear reference to the traditional place of the shipwreck and to the country villa of Publius. He also mentions the miraculous spring of water called *Fons Apostoli*, in Maltese, *Għajn Rażul*. He refers to the troglodyte cave-church of *Il-Madonna tal-Mellieħa*, where there is an ancient image of the Virgin Mary which was considered to be the work of Saint Luke, who was Paul's companion during his journey to Rome. In the ancient city of *Melítē*, which was known as Notabile or Medina during Ciantar's time (nowadays Mdina), the author mentions the Cathedral church of Malta, dedicated to Saint Paul, *Templum Cathederale, ubi sita erat antiqua Publii Domus*, that is, considered to having been built on the same spot where Publius had his house in the Roman town of *Melite*. Of particular importance for Ciantar is the *Crypta, quam Beatissimus Apostolus suae in hac Insula mansionis tempore frequentans, atque incolens illustravit*. This is the reference to Saint Paul's Grotto, just outside the walls of Mdina, which was a place of pilgrimage for many centuries, at least from the 14th century. Ciantar refers to the therapeutic nature of the rock of this crypt or cave-church, since during his time many samples were shipped from Malta and sent to Europe as relics of the same place where Paul had cured the Maltese and had rendered innocuous the venom of the viper. The fame of these relics, which were ridiculed by Đurđević as being pious inventions, is described by Ciantar. *Hinc eruitur mirificus ille contra venenos angues, morbosque*

[35] Giovanni Francesco Abela is considered to be the first Maltese historiographer. He was born in Valletta in 1582, son of Marco Abela and Bernarda Vella, who were members of the noble family of the Barone di Pietra Lunga. He studied history and literature, and rose to high ranks within the Order of Saint John, becoming Vice-Chancellor of the Order. He wrote various works in Italian and Latin, all of which were published in Italy, given that there was no printing press in Malta at the time. The most famous is *Malta Illustrata*, a description of the Maltese islands. Abela died in 1655 and was buried in the Church of Our Lady of Philermos, in the Conventual Church of Saint John in Valletta. He had acquired a *juspatronatus* in the Franciscan Church of Ta' Ġieżu (Santa Maria di Gesù) of the Observant Friars Minor, in Valletta, namely the chapel of Saint Trophimus (ex-chapel of Saint Januarius), which hosts a unique painting of Saint Paul healing the father of Publius, together with Saint Trophimus, who remained sick on the island, according to a mistaken tradition prevalent in Malta (Trophimus was sick in Miletus, not in Malta). The painting of the church altar is the work of Pietro Paolo Novelli, *il Monrealese* (1632). See Ġ. Aquilina (2011), 325-326.

lapis, vulgo dictus Grazia di S. Paolo, cujus virtus tota terrarum orbe pernota est. Ciantar also mentions the church of Saint Publius that had been built above the crypt, with the munificence of Grand Master de Wignacourt, as well as the church of Saint Paul and the cemeteries or catacombs spread all over this area, particularly the section known as *iz-zuntier ta' San Pawl*.[36]

The rest of this chapter is dedicated to the history of Malta and to the various monuments built during the reign of the Knights of Saint John, particularly the city of Valletta. Hence its relevance to our theme is marginal, except for the sections dedicated to the memory of Saint Paul. Overall, the aim of the author is that of glorifying Malta as it was governed by the Order of Saint John, and praising its prestigious role in Christian Europe.

A second section of Ciantar's volume is entitled *Series Episcoporum Melitensium*. As the title states, it aims at providing a complete list of the bishops of Malta, from the time of Publius to Fra Paolo Alpheran de Bussan (1728-1757). The list is artificially constructed and some of the names are historically dubious. Two things stand out, however, which are of interest to our theme, namely, the mention of Publius as first bishop of the island, and the interruption of the list of bishops of Malta during the Arab domination (870-1091) until the Norman conquest of the islands of Malta and Gozo. The thesis of Ciantar and many Maltese historians of the past regards the apostolic origins of the Church in Malta, thanks to the presence of Saint Paul who consecrated Publius, the *prōtos* of the island, as first bishop.

> "In the year 59 the Lord Publius, the chief man of Malta, who was more hospitable than Cydon of Corinth, after he had with great humanity welcomed and given hospitality to the Doctor of the Gentiles and his shipwrecked companions, was instructed in the rudiments of the Faith by the same Apostle, and was subsequently consecrated Bishop of the Church of Malta. Afterwards, he made great progress in the doctrine of the Gospel, under the discipline of St. Trophimus, who Paul left sick on this Island. After some years, around the year 67, when the Great Areopagite, Bishop of Athens, was sent to take care of new Churches, the same Apostle promoted him to the flourishing Episcopal See of Athens. He governed that Church in a praiseworthy manner, and crowned his life with martyrdom under the Emperor Trajan."[37]

The apostolic tradition of Malta is deeply rooted in the national consciousness and sensibility, and has been defended all along its history. During these last decades, some historians have cast serious doubts not only as to the apostolic origins of the Christian faith in Malta, but also as regards to the uninterrupted Christian tradition, particularly during the centuries of Arab domination. The opinion of contemporary Maltese scholars is that, although the Arab period brought with it an abandonment of the Christian faith by the majority of the population, and also the interruption of

[36] G.A. Ciantar (1738), 6-11.
[37] G.A. Ciantar (1738), 38.

the local hierarchy, various Christian influences remained and continued to thrive in Malta, and particularly in Gozo.[38] These were Byzantine influences, as was the framework of Christianity in Malta before the Latinisation of the islands after the Norman conquest. Ciantar belongs to the traditional view prevelant during the domination of the Knights of Saint John, which considered Malta to having been entirely Christianised by Saint Paul himself, who instituted the local hierarchy with Publius as first bishop, and the subsequent traditional list of bishops, many of whom, however, remain dubious during the first centuries of the ecclesiastical history of the islands.

We have already noted how Đurđević dismisses many of Ciantar's theses, or rather, the common opinion of Maltese historians at the time, regarding the memories of Saint Paul on *Melita Africana*. Indeed, as is evident from recent and contemporary studies, the historical origins of Christianity in Malta have needed to be redimensioned and not necessarily made to flow uninterruptedely from apostolic times. However, the evidence of Christian presence on the Maltese Islands is ancient, and the fact that Paul would have spent an entire winter on the island points to a great probability of his having evangelised the "barbarian" inhabitants of the islands, without necessarily pretending that a fully-fledged local Church was already present on Malta during the first century of the Christian era.

The various arguments treated by Ciantar

After the introductory chapters we have seen, Ciantar presents the plan of his work, made up of 20 *Dissertationes*, or Arguments. The structure is very similar to that of Đurđević, since it aims to respond to the latter's objections as to Malta's pride of place in having welcomed the Apostle of the Gentiles to its shores.

Ciantar presents also the Latin Vulgate version of Acts 27 and 28. This section is not as eruditely polished as that done by Đurđević who, as we have seen, presents the Greek original version, the Latin Vulgate edition, and his own translation. Undoubtedely Đurđević was much more prepared than Ciantar in his knowledge of the classical languages. The only noteworthy elements of this section regard the name of the typhonic wind, which Ciantar insists was the *Euroaquilo*, and the term *in locum Dithalassum*.

Of great interest is a rudimentary map of the place of the shipwreck according to the Maltese tradition. We shall return to this argument in a separate chapter. However, we can already note that this map sheds light on the prevailing tradition in Malta, that has been handed down to our present day. The map shows various

[38] J. Busuttil - S. Fiorini - H.C.R. Vella (2010), 166-169.

memories linked with the presence of Saint Paul in the vicinity of *Cala di San Paolo*, or Saint Paul's Bay. It depicts the church of Saint Paul and *Għajn Rażul*, or Spring of the Apostle, situated on the SE side of the bay. Further inland it represents the country villa of Publius, prince of the island, which has been identified, according to tradition, in the Roman remains of a country villa or agricultural establishment, at *San Pawl Milqi*, some 2 kilometres inland. It also mentions the church of *San Ġwann tal-Ħereb*, at Wardija, above the location of the villa, where it is held that Paul baptised the islanders in a baptismal font that used to be preserved outside a nearby church, *San Xmun ta' Wied Qannotta*, but which was simply a Roman stone olive-press trough. The map marks the Bay at Mellieħa, calling it *Santa Maria a Salinis*, and it pin-points the Sanctuary of *La Madonna della Melleha*, where the painting on the cave-church attributed to Saint Luke is venerated. Finally, it indicates the islet of *Selmunett*, which marks the whereabouts of the shipwreck, according to a more recent tradition, calling it *Scopulus Melitensibus dictus Selmun, D. Lucae Dithalassus*. Indeed, the actual place of the shipwreck in the map is not clearly indicated, since neither the islet of *Selmunett* nor the rocks at *Il-Blat tal-Għażżenin*, close to Saint Paul's church and Wignacourt's Tower, are universally accepted as being the actual places of the shipwreck. Instead, the map interestingly points to an underwater reef which is indicated as *Locus submissae bolidis, de quo Act c. 27 v. 28*. This reef does exist some metres away from the islet of Selmunett and could very well have been the place where the sailors made the soundings of the sea-floor before the actual shipwreck.

The first six *Dissertationes* deal with the issue of the name of the Sea of Adria which, as we have seen in the case of Đurđević's study, is the core issue of the whole shipwreck controversy. In the map we have just referred to, Ciantar calls it *Adriaticum-Siculum Mare, sive Ionium*. This confusion of names speaks volumes about the whole issue. The *Philomaltenses* were of the opinion that the Sea of Adria extended beyond the limited confines of the modern Adriatic Sea and covered the entire Ionian Sea from Sicily to Crete. Even Biblical scholars always held this view. Ciantar speaks about the Greek authors, who before Claudius Ptolemy would mix up the Sea of Adria with the Ionian or Sicilian Sea. He mentions the authority of Strabo, who extended the Adria Sea south and east of Sicily. Other authors also recognise the Sea of Adria in what was also called the Ionian or Sicilian Sea. Thus Ciantar is totally opposed to Đurđević, who wanted to limit the extent of the Adriatic Sea only to the sea extending from the Gulf of Venice to the Straits of Otranto, namely within the modern confines of the Adriatic Sea, where the island of Mljet is found and where he considered it a proof that the Apostle Paul was shipwrecked.

The seventh *Dissertatio* is dedicated to the typhonic wind which brought Paul's vessel to Malta (*Melita*), according to Ciantar, or to Mljet (*Meleta, Meleda*) according to Đurđević. The title states: "The typhonic wind which blew, as described by Luke, did not in any way take the ship of Saint Paul to Meleta (Mljet), but it could only drive it on towards Melita (Malta)." According to Ciantar, the question of whether the typhonic wind was the *Euroaquilo* or the *Euroklydōn* is irrelevant. He mentions various authors of antiquity regarding the discussion of the true nature and direction of the typhonic wind. As in the case of the Croatian Abbot, the conclusions drawn from these descriptions cannot be taken as a purely scientific analysis of the phenomenon, such as is nowadays possible for us to do. For Ciantar, the important thing is that the *Euroaquilo* wind blew Paul's ship from southern Crete towards the island of *Gavdos*; and thence towards the coast of Africa. The wind to which Luke refers blew in an ENE direction (*spirans inter Orientem, ac Septentrionem*) and not in an ESE direction (*flans inter Ortum, ac Meridiem*). Ciantar dismisses Đurđević's argument in favour of the *Euroklydōn* against the *Euroaquilo* by stating that the ship on which the Apostle was travelling was carried not to Dalmatia but to Malta, whatever the direction of the wind might have been.

As a proof of his thesis Ciantar publishes a letter by the noble Mario Lama, a Mathematician and cartographer, dated 27 December 1732 and written in Naples. The letter is an analysis on the extent of the Sea of Adria and on the typhonic gale. The arguments brought forth in the letter repeat, in many ways, what Ciantar had already stated, namely that the extent of the Adriatic Sea, according to ancient authors, would be much larger and would encompass the Ionian and Sicilian Seas, and that the typhonic wind could not possibly have been the *Scirocco*, or SE Levanter, but rather the *Gregale*, or NE Levanter, given that the position of Fair Havens and the island of *Gavdos*, or Cauda, off Crete, are good indications of the direction that the vessel would have taken, as well as the fact that it was tossed here and there for fourteen days and nights in the Sea of Adria. We shall see, obviously, that all these conjectures are not purely scientific, since at the time there was no detailed meteorological analysis of gales in the Mediterranean, and the exact location of the ports of Phoenix and Fair Havens mentioned by Luke in the diary log had been doubtful for many centuries, although nowadays our knowledge of both meteorological phenomena and locations of ancient cities and harbours in Crete has greatly improved.

The eighth *Dissertatio* deals with the "Barbarians, mentioned by Luke in Acts 28, who could be found living not in *Meleta* but in *Melita*." Ciantar does not agree with Đurđević, who regarded the inhabitants of Malta as Greek-speaking, and hence as not being Barbarians, given that the meaning of the term implies people who could not speak Greek (or Latin). In his description of Malta, Ciantar had dedicated many pages to the influence of Phoenician and Punic in the language of the Maltese inhabitants, although he does not reject that, for reasons of commerce and international contacts, the locals also spoke Greek and were regarded as Greeks. His thesis is strengthened by the fact that, although *Melita* was inhabited by Barbarians, Paul had evangelised these locals. He could not possibly have done so on *Meleta*, since the island was deserted and much of it was in ruins, and the remains present on the island did not go back to the times of Saint Paul. This was not the case of Malta, where there was a strong local community, governed by a *prōtos* and where Paul found fertile ground for evangelisation. The fact that the Maltese were Barbarians did not prohibit them from welcoming Paul's message and becoming fervent Christians.

The ninth *Dissertatio* is entitled: "Before the shipwreck of the Apostle and his arriving on the shores of Malta, there were neither innocuous serpents nor antidotes against their poison in the Maltese soil." Ciantar dismisses Đurđević's thesis that there were no poisonous serpents in Malta when Paul arrived, but that the venomous species of vipers lived on Mljet (*Meleta*). His arguments are varied and are not scientifically proven. Maybe the most interesting argument brought forward is that *Melita* lies south of Sicily and has a sub-tropical climate, whereas *Meleta* lies more to the north. Given that serpents thrive in hot climates, if one admits that *Meleta* was already infested with venomous vipers, how much more can this be affirmed in the case of sundrenched *Melita*! *Unde juremerito elicio, quod, si in parva Insula, ut est Melta, Septemtrioni subjacente, nascuntur mortiferi angues; multo magis in hac nostra, Austro subiecta, nasci ejusmodi serpentes deberent.* Ciantar arrives to the point of reasoning that a serpent could have bitten Paul because of the heat of the fire that aroused it, and its violent attitude might have been as deadly as poison (a kind of rabies), even if it were not a venomous viper. He also quotes other examples of other animals that could harm a person to the point of death with their bites, even if they did not transmit any poison. Another remote possibility brought forward is that the poisonous viper could have arrived with the same ship on which Paul was travelling, or could live on the island after having been transported with merchandise in the island's harbours.

The argument of the viper leads to *Dissertatio* 10, which deals with the Maltese *Glossopetre* or Stones which resemble the eyes of the serpents, and which were held to have hidden powers to cure persons from the poisonous bites of serpents. Ciantar admits that these are fossils, as are the teeth of an extinct megashark. We know that they belong to the *Carcharadon megalodon*, a probable ancestor of today's great white shark, *Carcharodon carcharias*. Ciantar dismisses many of the "scientific" opinions of his day, including some which Đurđević had embraced in order to ridicule the popular belief that Paul had rendered innocuous not only the serpents of Malta, but the same rocks of the islands, which abounded with these fossils.

Dissertatio 11 is dedicated to the *dithalassos*, namely, to the place of Saint Paul's shipwreck, on the island of *Melita*. Ciantar defends the Maltese ancient tradition of indicating the place of the shipwreck with the *Cala di San Paolo*, or Saint Paul's Bay. He explains the true nature of the "place between two seas", indicating that it was a piece of land which jutted out into the sea. The traditional place that was indicated since ancient times was the land that forms a shoal in the sea close to the church of Saint Paul, although the more popular, but more recent, tradition, places the shipwreck site on the islet of Selmunett, on the far side of Saint Paul's Bay. Although the whole complex issue is far from being resolved to this very day, Ciantar opts for the area of Saint Paul's Bay as the most probable site for the shipwreck, given that the country estate of Publius was also to be found close to the same bay. Ciantar also criticises his opponent Đurđević and challenges him to indicate with precision the actual place of the *dithálassos* on *Meleta* (Mljet), since he only speaks about "many" reefs near the Dalmatian island without any specific indication.

In the 12th *Dissertatio*, Ciantar tries to present proofs against three arguments of his opponent. The first argument regards the name *Melita*. According to Ciantar, all the Greek and Latin codexes coming before the Vulgate edition of Clement VIII, when dealing with the name of the island in the Acts of the Apostles, call it *Melita* or *Melitene*, and never apply this name to an island in Dalmatia. However, it seems that Ciantar admits that there was a whole confusion on the name of the island in question, since he quotes various authors who speak about *Militine, Mythelene, Melitussa* and other names as well. A second argument regards the political situation prevalent on *Melita Illyrica* and *Melita Africana* at the time when Paul was shipwrecked. While Malta seemed to enjoy prosperity under the Roman domination, Mljet was not known to be in very good terms with Roman supremacy, which had to subdue its rather belligerent inhabitants who used to plunder Roman ships in preceding centuries. Lastly, the question regarding the typhonic wind that brought Paul to the shores of *Melítē* is hardly a good indication of correct analysis of the direction towards which the *Euroklydōn* or *Euroaquilo* winds might have driven the vessel in which Paul was travelling.

The 13th *Dissertatio* is entitled: "The argument regarding Syracuse is for us particularly assisting, in spite of the unsuccessful attempts to disorient of the Adversary." Ciantar reminds the reader of what Luke states in Acts 28:11-13: "After three months we put out to sea in a ship that had wintered in the island - it was an Alexandrian ship with the figurehead of the twin gods Castor and Pollux. We put in at Syracuse and stayed there three days. From there we set sail and arrived at Rhegium. The next day the south wind came up, and on the following day we reached Puteoli."

Ciantar criticises Đurđević's position, when the Benedictine abbot stated that, since Syracuse is mentioned after Malta, it does not follow that Paul arrived there from *Melita Africana*. He could easily arrive from *Melita Illyrica*, more so because Alexandrian grain ships bound to Rome preferred to hug the coast and would go into the Adriatic and then would turn towards the heel and toe of Italy towards the Straits of Messina and proceed northwards. There was no impediment for a vessel to make a stop at Syracuse in Sicily, without any need for it to have wintered on the island of Malta. Ciantar quotes authors who state that this is a far-fetched opinion, since Syracuse is much closer to Malta than to Mljet. The ship would have travelled north, toward Messina, and not south toward Syracuse. This is a point in favour of Ciantar's thesis that the ship had wintered in Malta and travelled north to Sicily, and did not travel south from the Adriatic. Ciantar mentions Luke's accurate description of Paul's missionary journeys. How could it be possible that Luke would make Paul arrive from Mljet to Syracuse without mentioning the various places en route, including the Straits of Otranto, Taranto, and the Calabrian peninsula? Was it more logical to hold that Paul travelled from Malta to Syracuse by simply crossing the Sicilian channel, given that Luke states that a favourable southern wind carried the Alexandrian ship from Rhegium to Puteoli, and that probably it was the same wind that would bring it very easily from Malta to Syracuse?

Ciantar continues to present arguments in favour of his thesis in *Dissertatio* 14. He states that if the typhonic wind truly took Paul's ship to Mljet, since the island was scantily populated, the Centurion could find a return ship for the 276 passengers wintering in the port of Epidauros in the Adriatic (modern port of Cavtat in Croatia), and not on the island itself. With the words of the Flemish geographer and cartographer Petrus Bertius (1565-1529), Ciantar asks: *Quid enim navis Alexandrina, Syracusas petitura, faceret in littore Illyrico*? Ciantar quotes Đurđević himself who stated: *Quæ (Meleta) barbara, abstrusaque in Adriatico recessu, et inter tot insularum nomina, quibus Dalmatiæ littus prætexitur, fere demersa Orientalium navigantium cognitioni poenitus latitabat*. Therefore, if Mljet was unknown to oriental seafarers, how could it be that an Alexandrian ship would have wintered there? Again, how could Mljet have been the island of the shipwreck if there were no places of cult that gave witness to the presence of Paul on it, as there were in Malta, in the case of the Crypt of Saint Paul, for example? *Quid ergo est in caussa, cur in Dalmatensi Insula, nostra Æmula, nullum fuerit extructum Templum in Pauli Naufragi honorem*? Ciantar states that Mljet was inhabited by *Slavis, aut a Narentanis, feroci et Idolorum cultui addicta*! The ferocious inhabitants were idol worshippers and could not possibly have accepted the Christian faith and built places of cult. The fact that Đurđević defends the cult of Saint Paul on Mljet because of an image of the apostle which he states was present in a parish church and ridicules the Maltese tradition as too recent, is challenged by Ciantar who states that in Malta there are churches dedicated to many apostles, and yet this is not a proof that all of them ever came to Malta!

Dissertationes 15 and 16 are dedicated to the figure of Publius. Ciantar calls him "Saint Publius Martyr, Principal of Malta, who welcomed Saint Paul and became the first Bishop of Malta." He presents some authors of antiquity, who speak about the *prōtos*, or first citizen, of a Roman entity like Sicily, and states that the same could be said about Melita. Ciantar gives great importance to the Martyrologies that speak about Publius, and mention this name at various dates during the year. He states, with Abela, that Publius was born in Greece, and that he had been sent to Malta as a magistrate of the island together with his father, who was cured by Paul. Ciantar quotes the ancient inscription, mentioning a certain Lucius Prudentius who is called *Prōtos Melitaiōn*, the Chief man of Malta.[39] The country villa of Publius is also mentioned, as being situated not far from the village of Naxxar, a reference to the church of *San Pawl Milqi*, where the remains of a Roman agricultural establishment were discovered in 1960 by the Missione Archeologica Italiana a Malta.

Ciantar was aware of Đurđević's objection to the fact that Publius was ordained bishop by Paul, based on what 1 Tim 3:6 states regarding the fact that a newly baptised Christian was not to be consecrated bishop since he was still unprepared. Although accepting the objection, Ciantar quotes many examples of first-century bishops who were ordained by the apostles, particularly the case of Dionysius the Areopagite, chosen by Paul to be bishop of Athens. Ciantar states that, given Publius' prestige as *prōtos* of *Melítē*, together with his humility and generosity in welcoming the shipwrecked survivors, all point to excellent Christian qualities that could very well make of him a worthy leader of the first Christian community of *Melítē*. The case of Ambrose is a case in point, given that Ambrose was unanimously proclaimed bishop of Milan while he was still a catechumen. Another noteworthy example is that of Saint Martin of Tours, who according to Sulpicius Severus, gave his cloak to a poor beggar while he was still a catechumen, and was later elevated to the rank of bishop because of his great humility and charity. Ciantar reasons that it was not difficult to confer all the ranks of ministry in the Church to newly baptised Christians, elevating them to episcopal dignity. Obviously he is reasoning in a way that is nowadays unacceptable, since we know that the various ranks of ministry in the Church were by no means clearly defined during the first century. Publius was ordained bishop not only to preach the Gospel to the Maltese inhabitants, and thus continue the work initiated by Saint Paul, but also to be the leader of the Church in Malta. It is obvious that Ciantar wanted to present Publius as a fully-fledged bishop with ecclesiastical authority, having in mind the structural framework of a post-Tridentine Church more than that of a primitive Christian community.[40]

The ancient Roman Martyrologies have the following entry on 21 January: *ad 12 Kal. Febr. Athenis S. Publii Episcopi, qui Melitensis a Paulo Episcopus ordinatus*. The great devotion of the Maltese towards Publius was confirmed by the Church in September 1666, when it approved an *Officium proprium S. Publii Martyris, Episcopi Melitensis*.[41]

---

39 This inscription was first transcribed and translated by H.C.R. Vella (1980), 27.

40 As Roman Governor, Publius could not become Bishop of the Christian community. See H.C.R. Vella, *Malta u Għawdex fl-era klassika*, in *Kullana Kulturali* 38 (2002).

41 O. Bres (1872). Regarding the Divine Office of Saint Publius he writes: *Ed ecco Malta aver l'onore della Cattedra Vescovile fondata da un Apostolo ed aver avuto per suo primo Vescovo*

In *Dissertatio* 16 Ciantar dedicates his attention to the transfer of Publius to the Church of Athens. He quotes Bede the Venerable, who notes in his Martyrology: "Feast of Saint Publius, Bishop of Athens, who when he was Principal of Malta, during the time in which the Blessed Apostle Paul was travelling by sea to Rome, and was being held as a captive, received him kindly as a guest for three days, and treated him with rare human kindness, as Saint Luke writes. The father of the same Publius was suffering from fever and dysentery and was sick in bed. Saint Paul entered and placed his hands on him, and after praying, cured him. The same Publius became disciple of the Blessed Apostle and afterwards was consecrated Bishop. Paul sent him to preach. He shone with bright virtues and clear doctrine, and Christ crowned him with a glorious martyrdom. He was placed as Bishop in the See of Athens succeeding to Dionysius."[42]

According to tradition Publius was martyred either under the Emperor Trajan (112) or under the Emperor Hadrian (125). But according to another tradition, Saint Publius, Bishop of Athens, died in 171, during the time of Marcus Aurelius,[43] and according to Eusebius of Caesarea, he was not the direct successor of Dionysius the Areopagite, but of Narcissus. It seems that Đurđević followed this latter opinion, and Ciantar quotes him:

> "This same Publius, during the three months' stay of Paul, was adorned with the title of Bishop of the Maltese, when he was at least thirty years old. Now, according to the judgment of the Church, in order to be admitted to the office of Bishop, one had to be at least of this age, and at the same time (Publius) was governing the island of Malta as Magistrate. This happened around the year 56 (sic!) of the Christian era, during the time of emperor Nero when, as Jerome testifies, the Apostle went to Rome after he had been in Melita. Now Publius received his glorious Martyrdom as Bishop of Athens around the year 171 of the Christian era, that is, around the 10th year of emperor Marcus Aurelius. This corresponds to one hundred and fifteen years after the Shipwreck of Paul. If we count the thirty years of age of Publius before his episcopal consecration, we would arrive at one hundred and forty five years."

---

un Santo Martire, in cui onore sino dai più remoti tempi con somma divozione, e particolar vulto furono ivi eretti Templi, e Cappelle, si ottenne sin da' 14 aogsto 1666 dalla Sag. Congregazione de' Riti il permesso di recitare un'ufficio particolare in onore di S. Publio, nel quale si leggono le riportate in nota parole del Martirologio del Ven. Beda, e nel 1681 fu conceduta l'approvazione della Messa propria, che in Malta si celebra con somma pompa nei 21 Gennaro.

42 Venerable Bede, *Martyrologium Romanum*: *ad diem 21 Jan. Natale S. Publii Athenarum Episcopi, qui Princeps Insulæ Mileti cum navigantem B. Paulum humane tractasset ... Patrem ipsius Publii contigit febribus, et dissenteria vexatum jacere: ad quem cum intrasset Beatus Paulus, et imposuisset illi manus, et orasset, sanavit eum, quem Publium adhærentem sibi B. Paulus postea ordinatum Episcopum ad prædicandum direxit, et præclarus virtutibus, et doctrina præfulgens ob Christum martyrio gloriose coronatur. Nam prius Dionysius, deinde Publius iste Athenis præfuit.*

43 G.D. Gordini (1968).

It is obvious that, by following this tradition, Đurđević is trying to ridicule the position of Ciantar and of the *Philomaltenses* regarding the fact that the same Publius of Melita was also Bishop of Athens. According to more recent studies, we know that Đurđević's position has its value, although it is hard to pinpoint exactly to historical accuracy, given that the name Publius might have been common and that a confusion has certainly ensued in popular tradition and in the cult of this particular saint. Ciantar, however, defends his position and that of the Maltese, who venerated Publius in the church built above the Grotto of Saint Paul in Rabat, and he even arrives at stating that it is not surprising that a man could live well beyond a century and that, therefore, the Saint Publius Bishop and Martyr of Athens, could very well be the same Publius, *prōtos* of *Melítē*, who welcomed Paul in the island of Malta.

Dissertatio 17 deals with the case of Trophimus, whom Paul left sick on *Melita*, according to what he writes in 2 Tim 4:20. In modern translations of the Bible, the name is *Miletus*, not *Melita*. During the time when Ciantar wrote his dissertation, it was common opinion in Malta that Trophimus had accompanied Paul and Luke in the epic journey to Rome, and that he became sick on the island and was left there by Paul when the apostle proceeded on his journey to Rome after wintering on the island. Đurđević never accepted this opinion, and rightly so. The problem hinged upon the confusion of the ancient Greek name Μιλητος (*Milētos*).

The name *Milētos*, in Latin *Miletus*, refers to the ruins of *Milet* on the west coast of Turkey. *Milet* is the name of the city in modern day Turkey. It was an ancient Greek city on the west coast of Anatolia, near the mouth of the Maeander River in ancient Caria. Nowadays, these ruins are found close to the village of Balat in Aydin Province, Turkey. Acts 20:15-38 mention Miletus as the place where Paul met with the elders of the church of Ephesus in A.D. 57 at the end of his third missionary journey. The "Great Harbour Monument" records the place where this encounter is reputed to have occurred. It is in this town that Paul left Trophimus, his close collaborator, who was sick. But maybe it was not on this occasion, when Paul was returning to Jerusalem, but later on, during the period not recorded in the Acts of the Apostles, namely the year 65, when Paul returned to Miletus for a second visit. If this was the Miletus that Paul visited, then Đurđević might have a strong argument in favour of a probable presence of Paul on Mljet, since Paul was travelling in the whereabouts of the Aegean Sea, and could very well have visited the Epirus and Dalmatia.

The confusion of the names regards three Greek place names, namely Μιλητος (Mílētos), Μελίτη (Melítē), and Μυτιλήνη (Mutilḗnē, Mytilene). The first one is *Milētos* in modern day Turkey, the second one is *Melítē* (Malta, or Mljet), and the third one is *Mytilene*, the main town on the island of Lesbos. Ciantar continues to confuse things when he speaks about Miletus on the island of Crete (*qui Trophimum in Mileto Ionica, vel Cretica œgrotantema Paulo relictum*), maybe referring to the myth of *Miletos*, son of Apollo, or to the village of *Milatos*, close to the northern coast of Crete, some 45 kilometres east of Heraklion. Ciantar continues to follow the tradition, according to which, in the year 64, Trophimus went to Arles and became bishop of this city for thirteen years.

In the Franciscan Church of *Ta' Ġieżu*, in Valletta, Malta, there is a beautiful painting by Pietro Paolo Novelli, known as *il Monrealese* (1603-1647), depicting Saint Paul while he was in Malta, and who is in the act of curing Publius' father who was sick with dysentery. This is a unique painting in the chapel dedicated to Saint Trophimus (or rather, Saint Paul), in the Franciscan church, and its link with the family of Giovanni Francesco Abela indicates the strong local Maltese tradition that interpreted the name Miletus as referring to the island of Melita where Paul was shipwrecked.[44] Ciantar continued the tradition that Abela had initiated in Malta, particularly in his study *Malta illustrata*.[45]

---

[44] Ġ. Aquilina (2011), 325-326: "In 1625, the Vice-Chancellor of the Order and the first historiographer of Malta, Fra' Giovanni Francesco Abela, as he himself states, because of his devotion to Saint Francis and to the Franciscan Observant Order, had always desired to have a chapel in this church in order to be buried in and to bury his parents. The friars agreed to give to him, as the right of *patronatus* that he desired, the Chapel of Saint Januarius: *sita, aedificata et totalmente compiuta* (...) *dove al presente è situato l'altare e quadro di S. Gennaro Vescovo et Martire*. He agreed to donate 100 scudi to the friary, as one can see in the deed of this donation drawn in the acts of Notary Michele Ralli on 18 December 1625, after having obtained the permission of Grand Master Lascaris and that of the Holy See. This was necessary to avoid other legacies, now that he had acquired the *jus patronatus* of the chapel. It is interesting to give a look at some of the legacies that Fra' Giovanni Francesco Abela established in this church. These include Masses for his parents Marco e Bernardina Vella, other Masses for Gioacchino De Robertis and Marietta Abela De Robertis; a sung Mass on the feastday of Saint Januarius, since this chapel, as we have seen, was originally dedicated to this saint and not to Saint Trophimus; another Mass on the feast of Saint Clare, on 12 August, the day when his mother died, and a Mass on 21 October, the day when his father died; another votive sung Mass on 28 October, the day when Grand Master L'Isle Adam arrived in Malta, and on 28 March, commemorating this day in 1566 when *si diede principio alla fabrica e costruttione di questa humilissima Città Valletta*. Another sung Mass was to be celebrated on the feast day of Saint John the Baptist *per l'esaltazione e prosperità della Sacra Religione Hierosolimitana*. Giovanni Francesco Abela renamed this chapel in honour of Saint Trophimus, a companion of Saint Paul during his journey and shipwreck on our shores. In the *Descrittione di Malta*, after showing how Trophimus remained sick in Malta after Paul had left the island, according to information built upon the documentation of Cesare Baronio and the liturgical books of the Church of Arles, where it is said that Trophimus was the first bishop of that diocese, Abela concludes by stating: *Quindi è ch'ad honor suo, pochi anni sono nella Chiesa delli RR. Padri dell'Osservanza di S. Francesco di questa Città Valletta si fondò una Cappella, per insinuare altresì la memoria del Santo nella pietà de'nostri paesani*. On 12 April 1691, Canon Don Paolo Antonio Borg established another legacy of Masses on this same altar. The beautiful painting commissioned by Abela is attributed to Pietro Paolo Novelli, known as the *Monrealese*. It depicts Saint Paul who heals the father of Publius. Among the personages, there is Saint Trophimus. The painting bears the date 1632." English translation by the author of this study.

[45] G.A. Ciantar, *Malta Illustrata*, Vol. 3, 630: "Questo Trofimo per ragion di certa infermità non potè proseguire il viaggio coll'Appostolo, ma rimase nella nostra Isola, e non in Mileto."

Dissertatio 18 is entitled: "How we suspect that our adversary rashly concludes that the Maltese took over themselves the name of Christians late during their history." Ciantar mentions the opinion of Đurđević, who stated that there were remains of a temple dedicated to Juno in Malta (*Fanum Junonis* at Tas-Silġ),[46] that an inscription found on Gozo gave the title of *divus* to Emperor Antonius Pius, and that the Punic culture of the island was pagan. At the same time, Ciantar also reminds his readers that, in many other places where Paul preached the Gospel, it was difficult for him to abolish pagan cults, and yet one cannot say that Paul did not form Christian communities in such places as Ephesus. The fact that emperors continued to be proclaimed as *divi* should not surprise us, since even Saint Helena, mother of Constantine, called her son *divus* even when she became Christian. The titles *Divus, Divinissimums, Sanctus, Sanctissimus,* were often used to address persons in high authority both in the state and in the church, and they in no way indicated a pagan cult towards the same persons. So an inscription found in Gozo with this title does not mean that Malta was totally pagan and only accepted the Christian faith much later than apostolic times. As long as Malta was Roman, until Constantine, it was officially pagan.[47]

The last two *Dissertationes* of Ciantar's study regard the Traditions of the Maltese linked with the cult of Saint Paul. *Dissertatio* 19 is entitled: "The Maltese Traditions are praiseworthy and highly worthy of being believed." Although Đurđević tried to ridicule many of the Maltese Pauline Traditions, Ciantar insists on the veracity of historical evidence, particularly in his defence of the role of Publius in the Christianisation of the island of *Melítē*, which was continued throughout history by the list of bishops in communion with the See of Rome. Ciantar also defends all the local traditions of the Maltese, particularly those linked with the miracle of the innocuous nature of vipers on Malta and especially the fact that Luke states that Paul cured many of the islanders from various kinds of sickness. All these facts point to the truth of Paul's evangelising mission on *Melítē*.

Ciantar also tells his adversary: "It is true to all intents and purposes that no other Writer before Constantine Porphyrogenitus holds on to the statement that Paul was shipwrecked on the island of *Melita* of Dalmatia."[48]

The 20th and final *Dissertatio* is entitled: "Regarding the Monuments corroborating the Maltese Traditions, and especially the Pauline Crypt." Ciantar insists that, on Malta, there are various monuments which confirm the tradition of Saint Paul's shipwreck and his three-month stay on the island. He refers to his opponent Đurđević as suffering from the complex of the fox looking at the grapes in

---

46 M. Buhagiar (1996), 1-41.

47 H.C.R. Vella (1982).

48 G.A. Ciantar (1738), 411: *Verumenimvero nullus Scriptorum nullus ante Constantinum Porphirogennetem Pauli naufragium Melitensibus Dalmatœis adjudicavit.*

the fables of Aesop, since he could not boast similar monuments on Mljet. Ciantar boasts by stating: *Noster igitur, noster est Paulus Naufragus*.

Some distance inland from Saint Paul's Bay there were the estates of the first man of the island, Publius, who welcomed Paul and his companions, 276 persons in all. Ciantar indicates this place at *Benuerrat*, today known as *Burmarrad*, where the Maltese had built a church on the remains of a Roman agricultural estate or villa, known as *San Pawl Milqi*. On the hills directly opposite, overlooking the *Burmarrad* valley, stands the village of *Naxxar*. According to local tradition, confirmed by the coat of arms of this village, *Prior credidi*, the inhabitants of these hills were the first Maltese to accept the Christian faith preached by Paul. According to Ciantar, the name *Naxxar* derives from the Arabic *Nassara*, meaning Christians.

Close to the Roman establishment traditionally considered, without any historical foundation, to have been Publius' country residence, on the hills of *Wardija*, Ciantar indicates the church of Saint John, known as *San Ġwann tal-Ħereb*, where according to tradition Paul baptised Publius and many of the Maltese. We have already hinted at the "baptismal font" that was present near this church and for a time was located outside another church, that of *San Xmun ta' Wied Qannotta*, although according to the experts of the Italian Mission who conducted excavations at *San Pawl Milqi* in the 1960s, the nucleus for the tradition of Paul who baptised Publius should rather be located beneath the church of *San Pawl Milqi*, in the remains of the Roman country villa, which rendered that particular place sacred for many generations of believers.

Ciantar also refers to another tradition, always the result of popular belief but without any historical foundation, which states that, when the Norman Count Roger "freed" the islands from Saracen domination in 1090, the Maltese Christian slaves met him by singing *Kyrie, eleison* in *Wied ir-Rum*, which literally means *Vallis Christianorum*, the Valley of the Christians, from the Byzantine tradition *Rum*, meaning Christians. This is a valley overlooking the cliffs on the western coast of Malta.

Ciantar quotes John Chrysostom, who comments Acts 27:24: "God has graciously given you the lives of all who sail with you." He says that these words are a proof that Paul converted to Christianity not only his companions on the journey to Rome, but the islanders with whom he stayed on *Melítē* during the winter months of A.D. 60-61.

On the northern section of the island of Malta, above Saint Paul's Bay, Ciantar mentions another bay, *sinus a Salinis dictus*. The local name in Malta is *Mellieħa*. In the hills above the bay the Maltese still venerate an ancient rock painting of the Virgin Mary and Child in one of the troglodyte churches in this area. This place is nowadays a national sanctuary, known as *Il-Madonna tal-Mellieħa*. According to tradition, the icon of the Virgin and Child on the rock face was painted by Luke, companion of Paul during the journey to Rome and eye-witness of the shipwreck since the narration is included within the "we" sections of the Acts of the Apostles. Ciantar mentions the bishops who supposedly consecrated this Marian sanctuary in 416 on their way to the Council of Milevo near Carthage in North Africa (*Melivetanum Concilium*).

The most important shrine testifying to the presence of the Apostle Paul on *Melita* is the *Crypta Paulina*, or Saint Paul's Grotto, in Rabat. Ciantar first mentions the healing power of the rock powder taken from this Grotto, known as *Terra sigillata Melitensis*, a very popular but purely devotional talisman against snake-bites, which was exported in large quantities from Malta and sent all over Europe.[49] As we have seen, Đurđević had ridiculed this practice in his study. Ciantar mentions the sacred area around the Crypt, locally known as *iz-Zuntier ta' San Pawl*, where an ancient cross marked the place on which the Apostle would have preached to the Maltese. The place is marked by a stone mound and pedestal with the statue of the Apostle, a memorial built by the noble Maltese Lady Guzmana Navarra in 1678. Ciantar states that Paul would have resided in the Grotto or Crypt, and then would have preached the Gospel to the Maltese from this raised platform.[50] Ciantar accepts the theory that Paul was kept in relative captivity in the town of *Melítē*, but at the same time he states that from that place Paul could preach and cure many of the inhabitants who came to him. He accepts the far-fetched theory, ridiculed by Đurdević, that from that place Paul's preaching could be heard on the island of Gozo, and thus the inhabitants of the island of *Gaulos* were converted to Christianity.

Ciantar dwells also on the Cathedral church of Malta, situated in the old town of Mdina, the Arab equivalent form of the ancient Roman town of *Melítē*. According to him, the Cathedral was built on the same spot of the town palace of Publius, where the *prōtos* welcomed the 276 survivors of the shipwreck. In this church the Maltese venerate a very ancient icon of the Virgin Mary, said to have been painted by Saint Luke. Indeed, the icon is mediaeval in origin, and does not go back to the first centuries of Christianity, although a pious tradition also states that the icon was placed in the new Cathedral by the Normans after the previous one by Luke had been destroyed during the Arab domination of the islands. These are all conjectures that have no solid historical basis to be proven as true affirmations.

---

[49] G.A. Ciantar (1738), 426: *Hinc eruitur mirus ille, totoque Terrarum orbe celebratissimus lapis, albicans, gypsoque cocto similis, vulgo dictus "la Grazia di S. Paolo": cujus praesentissimam virtutem contra venenatorum animantium morsus, mortiferosque ex virulentia putredine morbos, jam satis in Dissert. 9 adversus Critici nostri opinionem evicimus.*

[50] G.A. Ciantar (1738), 429: *Nimirum prudentissimum gentium Doctorem, sicuti et alios Apostolos, tempus erat delitescendi, ac tempus coram hominibus versandi. Quum nempe Paulus Apostolicum suum ministerium exercere, gentibusque lucem afferre vellet, et spelunca egrediebatur, atque in hujus platea sive area (postea in cœmeterium conversa) Melitensi populo verba faciebat, et palam evangelizabat, imitans, ut Adversario placet, Magistrum suum, Christum Dominum: dicentem: "Ego palam locutus sum Mundo" (Joh 28,20).*

Ciantar concludes this important section with a direct attack on his adversary Đurđević, telling him that on *Melita Illyrica* he could not pin-point any of these momuments or traditions linked with the presence of Saint Paul. All evidence points towards *Melita Africana* as the island evangelised by Paul.[51]

Concluding remarks

Ciantar's study merits also the attention we have given to Đurđević's analysis of the Mljet theory, against the Malta theory that is generally accepted by biblical scholars. The period during which both authors composed their volumes saw a resurgence of interest on the location of Saint Paul's shipwreck. We have seen that it was during the first quarter of the 17th century that the cult of Saint Paul was revamped in Malta, thanks to the efforts of the Order of Saint John. Ciantar was a son of his age and culture. He was proud to be a native of the island that was evangelised by Paul, but also that was considered as a bulwark of Catholicism against the infidel Saracens. His rhetorical style, prevalent throughout the book, is a result of this sense of pride and prestige.

The author was simply replying to Đurđević's theory, expressed also in a polished but nearly arrogant style, and defending to the end the importance of Mljet as the island visited by Paul. We have seen both authors and examined their positions. We can say that both are rather biased about their ideas, and their style is polemical as a result. Yet both have their fair share of logical reasoning. Ciantar's position

---

[51] G.A. Ciantar (1738), 442-443: *En itaque multimodis dilutum, funditusque explosum Adversarii opinamentum, quo naufragum gentium Doctorem vel invitum in Meletam adigere conatus est. En sententiam nostram omnigenis rationibus, auctoritatibus, traditionibus, monumentis usquequaque sussultam, propugnatam, confirmatam: et maxime Apostolici Historiographi auctoritate, cujus verba, Pauli navigationem ac naufragium experimentia nulli sane alii quam Insulae nostrae conveniunt. Huc enim Adrianum mare jure suo perringit. Huc ventus Euroaquilo, sive Euriclydon a Creta navigantes impellit. Huic sinus cernitur habens littus a Paulinis Nautis conspectus. Ante hunc imum, ab illa tempestate Pauli nomine nuncupatum, videre est loca, in quæ bolidem ipsi submiserunt, ejusdem quidem profunditatis, quam recenset S. Evangelista. Heic locus dithalassus, atque Barbari erga Paulum sociosque humanissimi, ab illo memorati. Haud procul hinc Libycæ Syrtes, in quas incurrere illi meruebant. Huic Insulæ, Melitæ nomen, a Venerandi Interprete Vulgato constanter retentum, præcipue congruit. Hæc plana humilisque quum fit, a navigantibus eminus agnosci non potest. Heic serpentes præsentissimo veneno naturaliter imbuti erant. Heic reperiebatur Publius Melitensium Protus, qui naufragam illam catervam peramanter suscepit. Istius prædiorum, a Luca descriptorum, rudera adusque sæculum anteactum videbantur; et quidem ubi ea fuisse idem sacer Scriptor indicat. In hac Insula hyemare necessum erat; namque præ ceteris Adriatici Maris Insulis a Continente longe disjungitur. In hoc portu facillimum erat reperire Alexandrinam navem Puteolos transmissuram. Ex hoc portu abscessus versus Puteolos brevi occurrunt Syracusæ; indeque contendentis Romam iter eodem plane ordine, quo Lucas describit.*

was certainly better placed that Đurđević's, given that Mljet was never as densely populated as Malta, and the monuments commemorating a Christian presence on it are far fewer than the great number present in Malta. Nevertheless, it is very difficult to accept Ciantar's certainty that the Maltese traditions are proof of the veracity of Paul's presence on the island. Up to Constantine, Malta had to be officially pagan, and it practised Christianity underground, as in Rome. From recent studies we know that Christian presence in Malta can be dated to early Byzantine times, at least from the few remaining troglodyte places of cult on the island. What exactly happened before that is very much an object of conjecture, even though some of the conclusions that Ciantar makes have their degree of validity. It is indeed difficult to imagine the Apostle Paul staying on *Melítē* for three months and remaining idle, not proclaiming the Gospel. But the conclusions one takes on a devotional level are valid in their own sphere, and cannot be proven with historical documentation. Saint Paul was liberated by the very fact that he was shipwrecked. He was therefore never imprisoned in Malta, but was free to roam about.

The Mljet-Malta theories can only be examined in further detail with the help of contemporary evidence, particularly regarding the gale that could have carried Paul's vessel to either one of them. We have already spoken about Mljet. Now it is Malta's turn.

Chapter 4

The gale that carried Paul's ship from Crete to Melítē

The meteorological phenomena prevalent in the eastern and central Mediterranean during the late autumn and early winter provide us with the key to understand the facts narrated by Luke in the voyage diary that he wrote in Acts 27 – 28:14. We have already studied the interpretations given to this episode by two authors during the 18th century, who held widely differing opinions and theories, namely the Croatian Abbot Ignjat Đurđević, who defended the theory that Paul was carried from Crete into the Adriatic Sea and was shipwrecked on the island of Mljet, and the Maltese historian Giovanni Antonio Ciantar, who defended the more-accepted view that the gale carried Paul's ship from Crete to Malta. Given that these authors were writing at a time when the knowledge of meteorological phenomena was much less developed than it is nowadays, we cannot base our conclusions on their analysis, although they did produce erudite and well-presented studies, at least from the point of view of the historical and ancient documentary evidence. With the help of modern biblical exegesis and contemporary knowledge of meteorological phenomena in the eastern and central Mediterranean, we are in a position to trace the sequence of events as they occurred, even though Luke's intention was certainly that of providing a theological reading of them rather than a purely scientific or geographical interpretation.

In our analysis of the phenomenon of the gale or typhonic wind that carried Paul's ship to *Melítē*, we shall base our analysis upon Luke's account, although we repeat that it was not Luke's intention to speak of meteorological phenomena. The biblical studies on the journey of Paul to Rome are countless and it is not our intention to repeat what eminent biblical scholars have already stated. It is rather our intention to base our analysis upon two elements which can be of great help in tracing the correct course of events. The first one is a publication by James Smith, *The Voyage and Shipwreck of St. Paul*,[52] which is undoubtedly one of the best

[52] J. Smith, (1880). "At first glance, a Victorian sailor might seem an unlikely candidate to make a contribution to the study of the New Testament. And James Smith of Jordanhill was undoubtedly

contributions to the study of the art of seafaring, having been the result of personal experience of the author as an able seaman. Although it was written more than a century and a half ago, the book remains a valuable source of information regarding meteorological phenomena in the Mediterranean and the art of seafaring, as well as being a good analysis of Luke's account, since the author was well versed in Greek. The second element, which finds many confirmations in Smith's analysis, is my personal experience of the autumn and winter gales blowing on the island of Malta. Being an islander and having been a keen observer of meteorological phenomena on the coasts of my island home, like other Maltese, I have a personal experience of the typhonic ENE gale locally known as *Grigal*, from the Italian *Gregale*, which literally means a gale blowing from the direction of Greece. As we shall see, the term is normally understood to refer to a NE wind, which would presumably blow from the Peloponnese peninsula of Greece. In effect, the *Grigal* is not a NE wind. We shall examine this detail later on. The sight of the large waves breaking all along the north-eastern and eastern coast of Malta is an annual occurrence during the late autumn and early winter months and can last up to three consecutive days. The entrance and approaches to Grand Harbour and Marsamxett Harbour are spectacular on days like this, with waves going above the breakwater and spray rising as high as the upper reaches of Fort Ricasoli. The same can be said of the entrance to Saint Paul's Bay and the traditional place of the shipwreck on the islet of Selmunett, or else at Qawra point on the other end of the bay. On the east coast, the peninsula of Munxar at Saint Thomas Bay offers another spectacular sight, more so because of the extensive undersea sandy reef that goes out some

---

a sailor. Born at Glasgow in 1782 and educated at the University of Glasgow, Smith was one of the earliest members both of the Royal Yacht Club and one of the earliest commodores of the Royal Northern Yacht Club. His first voyage in his own vessel in 1806 was the beginning of a lifelong love affair with the sea. He took his last cruise in 1866, just a year before his death. But Smith was much more than just a sailor; he was also a keen student of ancient literature, a scholar who could read with facility not only Greek and Latin, but also most of the Romance and Teutonic languages, and a collector of rare books, particularly those relating to early voyages and travels. His knowledge both of geology and of archaeology was considerable, and on the subject of ships of the ancients he was a recognized authority. From 1839 to 1846, Smith was abroad—sailing, of course—and he wintered successively at Gibraltar, Lisbon, and Malta. It was his residence at Malta during the winter of 1844-45 that prompted the investigations that led to the research and publication of *The Voyage and Shipwreck of St. Paul*, which first appeared in 1848, when Smith was in his mid-60s. Smith argues persuasively that the shipwreck described in Acts 27-28 took place at the island of Malta. But he does much more than that. He shows, by a minute analysis of the text of Acts, by a very careful comparison with other descriptions of Mediterranean shipwrecks by Josephus and Lucian, and by a wide range of nautical information about prevailing winds, soundings, and coastlines, that Luke's account of the voyage and the shipwreck bears numerous marks of authenticity." (http://historicalapologetics.org/the-old-man-and-the-sea/ accessed 25 August 2017).

distance and creates a complex of currents in the area. All these phenomena point to two important details which we must consider, namely, the exact direction of the *Grigal* wind and the point where Saint Paul's ship could have been driven by the storm.

Our aim is not that of providing any conclusion of certainty regarding these matters. Many others have tried to do so before us and have not succeeded satisfactorily. Indeed, I think it is impossible to conclude exactly as to where Paul's ship foundered in Malta. Two thousand years have passed and the geological layout of the Maltese islands has been transformed, at least in places where the friable globigerina limestone has been easily eroded by sea action. Tectonic movements have also played their part in subsidence of parts of the coast, which maybe at the time when Paul was shipwrecked, were just below or above sea level. One thing has not changed, namely the yearly occurrence of the *Grigal* and the pattern of the typhonic wind that brought Paul's ship from Crete westwards to Malta.

Maybe one could state that the same wind could have carried the ship NW to Mljet in the Adriatic. This is another possibility that has to be examined, but I am not in a position to do it. Although I have visited Mljet personally twice, I have not experienced the Jugo SSE gales in the Adriatic. To come to the conclusion that Paul's ship entered the Adriatic is an assertion that needs more convincing proof.

Our analysis will proceed by following Smith's narration of the journey of Paul and his 276 companions from Caesarea on the coast of Palestine, to Sidon, and on to the port of Myra in modern day Turkey. The next leg of the journey saw Paul change vessel and embark on an Alexandrian grain ship on his way to Rome. The adverse winds made them arrive at Knidos, the south-westernmost tip of the Anatolian peninsula, and from there reach the island of Candia, or Crete, skirting it southwards by Cape Salmone (Akra Plaka) and proceeding along its southern shore to Fair Havens. An attempt to winter in the harbour of Phoenix by rounding Cape Matala ended in tragedy when a gale blew down on the coast from Mount Ida (Psiloritis) and led the ship out to sea towards the islet of *Gavdos*. From there the ship was carried westwards to *Melítē* (Malta) where it was shipwrecked at a point on the eastern or north-eastern coast of the island, in a place "between two seas" and in full view of a bay with a beach.

How could an ENE gale have brought Paul's ship from *Gavdos* to Malta? Should it not rather have led it, as Luke rightly states, on the Syrtis Banks in North Africa? Smith explains how the sailors managed to manoeuvre the ship in such a way that it was actually carried westwards along the deeps of the central Mediterranean basin between Crete and Malta, and above the Malta Escarpment that marks the beginning of shallower waters leading to the east coast of Malta.

The journey from Caesarea to Crete

In Acts 23:33-35, Paul is taken under strict Roman custody from Jerusalem to Caesarea Marittima on the Palestinian coast. It was A.D. 58, and Paul was under *custodia cautelaris* in Herod's *prætorium*, close to Herod's palace, in order to appear in front of the Roman governor, Marcus Antonius Felix, accused by the high priest Ananias and Tertullius, a Jewish lawyer, of having defiled the Temple by admitting Gentiles in it. Felix was succeeded by Porcius Festus, and left Paul imprisoned. In front of Festus, during a second trial, Paul, who was a Roman citizen, made an appeal to Caesar and thus Festus decided to send Paul over to Rome to be judged by the imperial tribunals. Caesarea was an artificial port constructed by Herod the Great in 21 B.C. Its remains have been unearthed and are now an Israeli National Park. The remains of the ancient harbour are still visible, and mark the place where Paul left in the early autumn of A.D. 60 on his fateful journey from Palestine to Rome.

In the company of other prisoners, Paul boarded a vessel under the direction of the centurion Julius of the Augustan cohort. The ship was from Adramyttium and was bound for the ports of the Roman province Asia. *Adramyttion* was a port on the west coast of Anatolia, between Troas and Assos to the west, and Pergamum to the south, facing Mitylene on the island of Lesbos. Nowadays it is called Edremit in Turkey. The first leg of the journey was along the coast of Palestine, due northwards, towards Sidon, an important port of Phoenicia, where Julius allowed Paul to go and visit his friends.

From Sidon the journey continued northwards. Acts 27:4-5 state: "From there (Sidon) we put to sea again, but as the winds were against us we sailed under the lee of Cyprus, then across the open sea of Cilicia and Pamphylia, taking a fortnight to reach Myra in Lycia." What exactly does Luke mean when he states that the ship "sailed under the lee of Cyprus" (ὑπεπλεύσαμεν τὴν Κύπρον)? We know that, in Paul's time, voyages by sea were normally accomplished by following the coasts and possibly avoiding open sea, where dangers for navigation were much greater. If the winds were contrary, we understand that they were westerly winds, hitting the vessel head on. In order to avoid these winds, the ship passed "under the lee" of Cyprus. This expression might mean that it journeyed *south* of Cyprus. Smith does not agree with this theory and proposes his own, namely, that the ship passed to the *north* of Cyprus, through the sea of Cilicia, having the land breezes coming from the Anatolian peninsula to help it in making headway against the oncoming westerly winds.[53]

---

[53] J. Smith (1880), 26-28: "When we hear of contrary winds, and wish to ascertain their direction, the chief points to be determined are the ship's actual position and intended course. Now, when Saint Luke talks of contrary winds, we know that the ship had left Sidon, and must have been

Their journey from Sidon took them due NNW around Cape *Apostolos Andreas*, the easternmost tip of Cyprus, and then due WNW, having Cyprus on their left and the Anatolian land mass on their right. Thus, they proceeded with difficulty towards the next port of their journey, and after 15 days they reached the port of Myra in Lycia (modern Demre in Turkey). It was at Myra that the company changed ship. The vessel they had boarded in Caesarea was only fit to ply between the coastal ports of Asia Minor and Palestine and could not face the open seas between Greece and Italy. For this reason, the centurion found an Alexandrian grain ship leaving for Italy. The Roman Empire was constantly in need of enormous quantities of grain, and we know that wheat was grown in abundance in the regions of *Africa Proconsolaris*, *Cyrenaica* and *Ægyptus*, in what is nowadays largely desert. From the port of Alexandria large grain ships would sail for Italy, possibly avoiding the hazards of crossing the *Mare Internum Nostrum* (Mediterranean Sea) directly WNW to the Straits of Messina and northwards along the *Mare Tyrrhenicum* to Puteoli and Naples. They would rather cross the eastern Mediterranean directly northwards to Lycia[54] and then cross the *Mare Ægeum* to Achaea and follow the coast of Epirus, going over across the *Mare Ionium* to Rhegium and into the Straits

---

in sight of Cyprus, for he tells us the winds forced them to leeward of that island. Their ultimate object was Italy, and their proximate one was one or other of the 'places in Asia', which I have already shown lay in the same direction. As Saint Luke does not include Pamphylia in Asia, the nearest part of that region to Syria is Lycia, and a ship's course from Sidon thither is W.N.W., leaving Cyprus on the right. St. Luke was perfectly aware of this, for upon the former voyage, in which he accompanied Saint Paul, he tells us that on their passage from Patara, one of the 'places in Asia', to Phoenicia, they left Cyprus on the left hand, *i.e.* on the north. (Acts xxi.3). The winds, therefore, which prevented them from taking the straight course to the places in Asia must have been from the westward. Now these are the very winds which might have been expected in this part of the Mediterranean at this season (summer). Under these circumstances, sailing under Cyprus is equivalent to saying that they left Cyprus on their left hand; but this point is put out of doubt by Saint Luke himself, for he tells us in the 5th verse that they *sailed through* the sea of Cilicia [...]; but as this sea lies altogether to the north of Cyprus, they could not have sailed through it without leaving the island on their left. In pursuing this route they acted precisely as the most accomplished seaman in the present day would have done under similar circumstances; by standing to the north till they reached the coast of Cilicia, they might expect when they did so to be favoured by the land breeze, which prevails there during the summer months, as well as by the current, which constantly runs to the westward, along the south coast of Asia Minor."

[54] J. Smith (1880), 32-33: "Now it is quite true that Myra is out of the direct course from Alexandria to Italy, which is by the south of Crete. But with the westerly winds which prevail in those seas, ships, particularly those of the ancients, unprovided with a compass, and ill calculated to work to windward, would naturally stand to the north till they made the land of Asia Minor, which is peculiarly favourable for such a mode of navigation, because the coast is bold and safe, and the elevation of the mountains makes it visible at a great distance; it abounds in harbours, whilst the sinuosities of its shores and the westerly current would enable them, if the wind was at all off the land, to windward, at least as far as Cnidus, where those advantages ceased."

of Messina. It is for this reason that Đurđević insisted that the course taken by Paul's ship was intended to bring it into the Adriatic and on to Dalmatia, where it ended up shipwrecked on the island of Mljet. This direction would, however, have taken the ship totally off course and would create an unnecessary detour in order to cross the Straits of Messina, without, of course, forgetting that the gale-force wind that it encountered off Crete could not possibly have driven it into the Adriatic, but rather across the *Mare Siculum* due W towards Malta.

The first leg of the journey from Myra was a difficult one. "For some days we made little headway, and we had difficulty in making Cnidus" (Acts 27:7). The way from Myra to Cnidus was due NW, directly facing the wind. That is why Luke states that they made little headway. The ship sailed close to the coast until it arrived in the straits between the mainland and the island of Rhodes. Going further west past the island of Simi the ship would arrive at the westernmost point of the Datça peninsula where the town of Cnidus stood, at the entrance to the Aegean Sea. Cnidus was an ancient Greek city of Caria.

The ship could not enter for safety at Cnidus. "The wind would not allow us to touch there, so we sailed under the lee of Crete off Cape Salmone and struggled along the coast until we came to a place called Fair Havens, near the town of Lasea" (Acts 27:7-8). The course that the vessel should have followed was that of turning due SW towards the island of Karpathos and then reaching the northernmost tip of Crete at the Kyriamadi peninsula and turning due West along the northern coast of the island, having the Aegean Cyclades islands and then the Peloponnese peninsula to their right, through the Sea of Crete. Instead, the strong westerly winds forced them to change course and turn south along the east coast of Crete, facing Salmone, today known as Akra Plaka peninsula, and then continuing along the southern coast of Crete, protected by the island itself, until they would arrive at the port of Fair Havens, which was the most western safe haven before Cape Matala.[55]

The position of Fair Havens, according to Smith, is rather doubtful, more so because no remains of the town of Lasea have been found in this region of southern Crete. However, there is a bay in southern Crete which is closest to Cape Matala and fits the description of Luke in Acts. This is the bay of *Kaloi Limenes*, which is precisely the Greek name for Fair Havens. This bay is open to the easterly winds but protected from the west, and moreover has two tiny islands, Megalonisi

---

[55] J. Smith (1880), 42-43: "After working up along the southern coast of Crete, they reached Fair Havens, which we have seen is the farthest point which an ancient ship, navigating under the lee of Crete, could reach with north-west winds. As this is an important point in the voyage, it becomes necessary to ascertain precisely its situation, as well as that of the port of Phoenice and the island of Clauda. Saint Luke marks the position of Fair Havens by its vicinity to the city of Lasæa; but neither Fair Havens nor Lasæa are noticed by any other ancient author, nor have the ruins of the city been discovered in modern times."

and Mikronisi (Saint Paul Islet), which protect it from the southeast. Although nowadays it is not much more than a sandy beach, it could have provided good anchorage during the 1st century A.D.

It was at this point that Paul admonished his comrades in navigation that it was now too late to continue on their journey, since navigation in the Mediterranean was prohibited from late autumn to early spring.[56] "A great deal of time had been lost, and navigation was already hazardous, since it was now well after the time of the Fast, so Paul gave them this warning: 'Friends, I can see this voyage will be dangerous and that we will run considerable risk of losing not only the cargo and ship but our lives as well'" (Acts 27:9-10). The Fast corresponds to the Jewish Festival of *Yom Kippur*, the Day of Atonement, which falls on 10 Tishrei of the Jewish Calendar. Now, in the year 59 A.D., 10 Tishrei (of the Jewish year 3820) fell on 5 October, whereas in the year 60 A.D. it fell on 24 October.[57] Since it was "well after the time of the Fast", we can state that the Alexandrian grain ship anchored at Fair Havens roughly around the end of October or beginning of November 60

---

[56] O. Tammuz (2005), 145-162. In p. 146 the author presents the description of the navigational seasons by Vegetius (4th century AD): "The violence and roughness of the sea do not permit navigation all year round, but some months are very suitable, some are doubtful, and the rest are impossible for fleets by law of nature. When Puchon has run its course, that, is, after the rising of the Pleiades, from six days before the Kalends of June (27 May) until the rising of Arcturus, that is, eighteen days before the Kalends of October (15 September), navigation is deemed safe, because thanks to the summer the roughness of the sea is lessened. After this date until three days before the Ides of November (11 November), navigation is doubtful and more exposed to danger, as after the Ides of September (13 September) rises Arcturus, a most violent star, and eight days before the Kalends of October (24 September) the rainy Haedi, and five days before the Ides of the same (11 October) Taurus. But from the month of November the winter setting of the Vergiliæ (Pleiades) interrupts shipping with frequent storms. So from three days before the Ides of November (11 November) until six days before the Ides of March (10 March) the seas are closed. The minimal daylight and long nights, dense cloud cover, foggy air, and violence of the winds doubled by rain and snow not only keep fleets from the sea, but also traffic from making journeys by land. But after the birthday, so to speak, of navigation which is celebrated with annual games and public spectacles in many cities, it is still perilous to venture upon the sea right up to the Ides of May (15 May) by reason of very many stars and the season of the year itself – not that the activities of merchants cease, but greater caution should be shown when an army takes to the sea in warships than when the enterprising are in a hurry for their private profit."

[57] A.M. Buscemi (1997), 228, footnote 111: "Prendendo, infatti, come punto di riferimento lo Yom Kippur (At 27,9), la partenza da Boni Porti sarebbe avvenuta verso il 5 Ottobre (59 d.c.), una data pericolosa per la navigazione, ma non del tutto impossibile. Mentre se si prende come punto di riferimento lo Yom Kippur dell'anno 60, allora la partenza sarebbe avvenuta verso il 24 Ottobre, una data veramente pericolosa per intraprendere un viaggio e che spiega l'insistenza di Paolo a non partire. Significativo quanto affermava Vegetius, *De Re Militari*, 4,39: la navigazione è sicura fino al 14 Settembre, diviene incerta fino all'11 Novembre, da questa data fino al 10 Marzo il mare è chiuso."

A.D., when navigation was becoming truly hazardous. This is the reason why Paul admonished his comrades to stay put at Fair Havens during the winter months.

However, neither Julius nor the ships' captain heeded Paul's admonitions. "But the centurion took more notice of the captain and the ship's owner than of what Paul was saying; and since the harbour was unsuitable for wintering, the majority were for putting out from there in the hope of wintering at Phoenix – a harbour in Crete, facing south-west and north-west" (Acts 27:12-13).

Paul was not a seaman, but he had certainly travelled far and wide, and had met many dangers during his journeys by land and sea.[58] So, in some ways, he was an expert in having a premonition of what was inevitably going to happen.[59]

The ship's commanders therefore decided to take the vessel to a safer harbour. According to Smith this was Loutro, on the south coast of Crete, but further to the west. Indeed, in order to arrive at Loutro (Phoenix), they had to go out of Fair Havens, round Cape Matala, and direct the ship's course due NW, since at that point the coast abruptly turns north and then west. During the crossing, which should have been relatively easy and short, the ship would pass close to two tiny islands, known as *Paximadia Dyo* and *Paximadia Ena.*

---

[58] 2 Cor 11:24-26: "Five times I have been given the thirty-nine lashes by the Jews; three times I have been beaten with sticks; once I was stoned; three times I have been shipwrecked, and once I have been in the open sea for a night and a day; continually travelling, I have been in danger from rivers, in danger from brigands, in danger from my own people and in danger from the gentiles, in danger in the towns and in danger in the open country, in danger at sea and in danger from people masquerading as brothers."

[59] J. Smith (1880), 47-48: "It was determined at this consultation to attempt to reach Phoenice, a harbour of Crete, which looked, according to Saint Luke, κατὰ λίβα καὶ κατὰ χῶρον, which is rendered in our version, 'lieth toward the south west and north west.' The intermediate point between these two winds is west; and it is generally understood that the harbour looked to, or was open to, the west. Father Giorgi, aware that if it could be proved Phoenice was on the south side of Crete, a ship could not be driven off the island towards the Adriatic Gulf, infers from this that it was at the west end of the island, and that the situation of Clauda is uncertain. Dr Falconer, a man of undoubted learning, admits that it is not easy to determine the exact import of this passage, but supposes it to be 'open to both quarters of the heavens from whence these winds proceed, and of course unsheltered from these winds:' he then observes that 'this would, according to Vitruvius, leave 150^0 open to the west. Such a harbour would certainly not be 'commodious to winter in,' and would not have warranted the attempt which was made to move to it.' Although they never reached this harbour, it becomes of importance to ascertain its position; because, unless we do so, we can draw no sound inferences respecting the ship's place when she encountered the gale, a point which it is of importance to determine. Phoenice no longer retains its name; there is, indeed, a place named Phoenikias in Pashley's map, not far from the position assigned to it by Strabo and Ptolemy; but this cannot be the port of Phoenice, for it is not on the coast; although it may possibly be the city of that name, for Ptolemy mentions both a city and port of Phoenice, or rather Phoenix. Loutro, Sphakia, and Franco Castello, places on the south coast of Crete, have each been supposed to be Port Phoenice. For our present purpose of ascertaining the ship's course, it is not very material which of them is meant: I am, however, satisfied that it is the harbour of Loutro."

The problem with the description of Phoenix (Loutro) is that Luke states that it was "facing south-west and north-west". Now, Smith states that Loutro looks to the east. So, how does one explain the seemingly contradictory directions? According to the same Smith:

> "the words of St. Luke in the original are generally supposed to indicate a harbour open in the opposite direction [...] I apprehend it means '*in the same direction as*' (in Latin, *secundum*); if I am right, [it ...] does not mean, as is generally supposed, that it is open to the point *from* which the wind (Libs) blows, but to the point *towards* which it blows – that is, it is not open to the south-west but to the north-east."[60]

If one looks closely at a map of Loutro Bay, one notices that it looks east. It is well sheltered from the NW gales by a strip of land behind it, and from the SW gales by a tiny island having its same name. However, it would have been completely at the mercy of the waves coming from a strong Levanter wind, namely an ENE gale. For Julius and the ship's crew, however, it seemed the most sensible decision to winter here, in this port of Phoenix, rather than remain in Fair Havens (Kaloi Limenes), which was more prone to the effects of SW gales. No harbour on the southern coast of Crete was totally suitable to winter in, but the company had no choice, and preferred to take the opportunity of a fair southerly breeze to make it to Phoenix. They rounded Cape Matala, and tragedy struck.

The gale from Crete to *Melítē*

> "A southerly breeze sprang up and, thinking their objective as good as reached, they weighed anchor and began to sail past Crete, close inshore. But it was not long before a hurricane, the 'north-eastern' as they call it, burst on them from across the island" (Acts 27:13-14). [13 Ὑποπνεύσαντος δὲ νότου δόξαντες τῆς προθέσεως κεκρατηκέναι, ἄραντες ἆσσον παρελέγοντο τὴν Κρήτην. 14 μετ' οὐ πολὺ δὲ ἔβαλεν κατ' αὐτῆς ἄνεμος τυφωνικὸς ὁ καλούμενος εὐρακύλων].

It is here important to understand the meteorological phenomena that gave rise to the hurricane wind in such a sudden and unexpected way. Luke states that a "southerly breeze sprang up." The direction of the breeze is from Cyrenaica in Libya. This means a southern wind blowing from the Sahara and Libyan coast across a short stretch of sea, carrying with it a high relative humidity. It is quite normal to have *Scirocco* winds in the eastern and central Mediterranean during the first half of autumn. Indeed, these winds are fundamental in bringing the optimal conditions for the autumn rains which are so precious in the semi-arid islands of the Mediterranean. In Malta, the hot and humid winds blow either from the

---

[60] J. Smith (1880), 49.

SW (Tunisia), or S (Libya) or SE (Cyrenaica), whereas in Crete we find the same phemomenon of hot and humid winds coming from the S and SE. What normally occurs in the case of Crete is that these hot and humid winds meet colder air masses coming down from the Balkans, and create a kind of micro-climate that is unique in its own right. The reason is that, some kilometres above Cape Matala, we find the highest mountain on Crete, namely, Mount Ida (in Greek nowadays called *Psiloritis*), going up to a height of 2,456 metres above sea level. It was considered to be sacred to the Greek Titaness Rhea, mother of the gods, and on its slopes lies a cave, *Idaiōn Andrōn*, in which, according to legend, Zeus, the youngest son of Rhea, was born. There is a small church dedicated to the Holy Cross (*Timios Stavros*) on its peak, which has the highest topographic prominence in Greece.

The rapid elevation of Mount Ida, which lies barely 20 km from the coast north of Cape Matala, was the reason for the sudden change of meteorological conditions. The hot and humid African wind soon met the cooler air masses high on Mount Ida, and this would give way to a stormy cyclonic condition described by Luke as a "hurricane" which "burst upon them from the island." The ship was in the *Hormos Mesaras*, a large bay west of Cape Matala, crossing due NW towards Loutro, maybe close to the islets of *Paximadia Dyo* and *Paximadia Ena*, when it encountered a strong gale coming down from Mount Ida in an ENE direction, which Luke calls *Euroaquilo* (some versions have *Euroclydōn*), a combination of two Latin terms meaning east and north.[61] This is the origin of the autumn gales that normally blow from mid-October to the beginning of December (in some rare instances even beyond, in January),[62] that are the result of the meeting of hot and humid air masses from Africa with cooler air masses from Europe (in this case from the Balkans), and which blow with great strength (Force 8 and beyond) over the entire stretch of sea extending from Crete to Sicily and to Tunisia, and which are locally known as *Gregale* in Italian and *Grigal* in Maltese.

---

[61] J. Smith (1880), 59-60: "The sudden change from a south wind to a violent northerly wind is a common occurrence in these seas. The term *typhonic*, by which it is described, indicates that it was accompanied by some of the phenomena which might be expected in such a case, namely, the agitation and whirling motion of the clouds caused by the meeting of the opposite currents of air when the change took place, and probably also of the sea, rising it in columns of spray. [...] Saint Luke, therefore, by the single word 'typhonic,' expresses the nature and violence of the gale, and, by another, its direction. In the dissertation on the wind Euroclydon, I have stated my reasons for preferring the reading of the most ancient manuscripts and versions, Euro-aquilo, which must be between Eurus and Aquilo, or E.N.E."

[62] On 24 January 2008 Malta witnessed a particularly strong off-season NE gale. According to weather records from the Met Office in Malta International Airport, on 24 January 2008, the direction of the wind was NE, with maximum gusts of 74km/H. Another very strong storm was experienced on 2-3 December 1989, during the George Bush – Mikhail Gorbachev summit in Malta. On 8 December 1988, a strong *Gregale* storm hit the Maltese islands.

> "The ship was caught and could not keep head to wind, so we had to give way to the wind and let ourselves be driven. We ran under the lee of a small island called Cauda and managed with some difficulty to bring the ship's boat under control" (Acts 27:15-16). [συναρπασθέντος δὲ τοῦ πλοίου καὶ μὴ δυναμένου ἀντοφθαλμεῖν τῷ ἀνέμῳ ἐπιδόντες ἐφερόμεθα. νησίον δέ τι ὑποδραμόντες καλούμενον Καῦδα ἰσχύσαμεν μόλις περικρατεῖς γενέσθαι τῆς σκάφης].

The full force of the gale pushed the ship out to sea in a SW direction. Ancient ships could not face the wind particularly if caught in a gale, and the only temporary solution was to let themselves be carried adrift. The initial direction of the wind, coming from the NE, took them directly towards a tiny island, called *Gavdos* (Cauda in the Bible).

Gavdos is a small island (32.4 km^2), situated some 48 km off the southern coast of Crete. It is the most southern of the Greek islands and marks the southernmost tip of the European continent, facing the coast of Cyrenaica in Libya. In antiquity it was known by various names. In Acts Luke calls it *Clauda* or *Cauda*. Ptolemy called it *Klaudos*. The Venetians called it *Gotzo*. Its name, *Gavdos*, italianised in *Gotzo* or *Gozzo*, confuses it with the island of Gozo near Malta, which is locally called *Għawdex*, a Semitic transliteration of the Greek name *Gavdos*. There is a small islet called *Gavdopoula* to the northwest of Gavdos.

The ship carrying Paul and his comrades was driven in the direction of this island, and they succeeded in rounding its southernmost tip and finding shelter in the lee of the island, which is ideally suited for protection against the ENE gales since it is made up of cliffs running from the southeast to the northwest tip of Gavdos.[63]

Smith describes with minute detail the art of seamanship in ancient shipping, and in this particular case, and a reference to his expert description would be of great help in understanding exactly how things occurred during the storm. Protected, at least temporarily, by the lee side of Gavdos from the onslaught of the ENE gale, the sailors took all necessary precautions to prepare the ship for the further challenge

---

[63] J. Smith (1880), 60-61. 63-64: "I now proceed to inquire into the effects it produced upon the ship. Nothing more is said in the narrative than that it defeated their object of reaching Port Phoenice, and forced them to run under the lee of Clauda. It will, however, be found that the ship must have strained and suffered severely in her hull, and that the leaks she then sprang were gradually gaining upon the crew, and that if they had not providentially made the land, and been thereby enabled to save their lives by running the ship on shore, she must have foundered at sea, and all on board perished. [...] At the time the ship was caught in the gale, she must have been near a small group of islands, called the Paximades, in the Gulf of Messara. The island of Clauda lay about twenty-three miles to leeward, and thither they were driven, as the expression ἐπιδόντες ἐφερόμεθα (v. 15) implies, before the gale. Upon reaching it, they availed themselves of the smooth water under its lee, to prepare the ship to resist the fury of the storm. [...] I conclude that they passed round the east end of the island; not only because it was nearest, but because there are dangers at the opposite end."

that lay ahead. They could not possibly stay put in that position. The coast offered no natural harbours, Gavdos was an island off the beaten track, there was no food to survive the winter months even if they could make it to land. Their only option was to force the way ahead in the midst of the fury of the storm. In order to do so they had to prepare the ship. As we said, if they let the ship drift at the mercy of the storm by being carried forward without any control (technically "to scud", to run before a gale), this would have led them to disaster. Straight ahead lay the North African coast of Cyrenaica, where part of the Syrtis Banks are located. They would certainly have been shipwrecked and perished on those shoals. So, what they did was to try to get the vessel go adrift, but not in an ENE direction at the mercy of the wind, but rather to take it out to open sea due westwards. In order to do so, they had to turn the ship's prow as much as they could towards the N, in such a way that the ship's starboard would take the full force of the waves at an angle. This would mean that the ship would heave and roll dangerously, but that it would slowly drift westwards towards the coast of Sicily. They had no way of knowing that the wind would carry them to the island of Malta, which lies due WNW at a distance of 513 nautical miles (950 kilometres) from Kaloi Limenes on Crete to Marsaxlokk, the closest bay on the SE coast of Malta. As we shall see, they were to take 14 days to cross this stretch of sea, to be more exact some 13 days if we consider the first day lost preparing the ship when they were caught in the storm and halted in the lee of Gavdos.

> "As we were thoroughly storm-bound, the next day they began to jettison the cargo, and the third day they threw the ship's gear overboard with their own hands. For a number of days both the sun and the stars were invisible and the storm raged unabated until at last we gave up all hope of surviving. Then, when they had been without food for a long time, Paul stood up among the men. 'Friends,' he said, 'you should have listened to me and not put out from Crete. You would have spared yourselves all this damage and loss. But now I ask you not to give way to despair. There will be no loss of life at all, only of the ship. Last night there appeared beside me an angel of the God to whom I belong and whom I serve, and he said, 'Do not be afraid, Paul. You are destined to appear before Caesar, and God grants you the safety of all who are sailing with you.' So take courage, friends; I trust in God that things will turn out just as I was told; but we are to be stranded on some island'" (Acts 27:18-26).

The fact that the sailors could see no stars at night, because of the overcast skies, means that the ship was totally lost in its bearings. At this point, the author of the narrative inserts a theological reflection upon God's provident care on the stricken crew and passengers. It is important to note, as we have already stated, that the aim of Luke in the Acts is that of giving a theological reading of the history of the evangelisation of the early Church "not only in Jerusalem but throughout Judaea and Samaria, and indeed to earth's remotest end" (Acts 1:8). The journey of Paul to Rome marks the culmination of his apostolic ministry to the remotest ends of the earth. Although Paul could very well have continued to evangelise regions even beyond Rome (tradition ascribes to him the evangelisation of Spain and Illyricum), the scope of Acts was precisely that of making Paul arrive at the centre of the known world and there proclaim Jesus Christ. So, the account of the gale and shipwreck should be seen within the context of this providential plan of God to bring Paul to give witness to Jesus in Rome. The stop-over in Malta, a result of the contingent forces of nature, becomes part and parcel of God's plan, and we shall see how Paul took advantage of this time and opportunity to make known the wonders of his evangelising ministry even among the "barbarians" of *Melítē*. Paul "was destined" by God to appear before Caesar, but he was also destined to be "stranded on some island" in the meantime.

> "On the fourteenth night we were being driven one way and another in the Adriatic, when about midnight the crew sensed that land of some sort was near. They took soundings and found twenty fathoms; after a short interval they sounded again and found fifteen fathoms. Then, afraid that we might run aground somewhere on a reef, they dropped four anchors from the stern and prayed for daylight. When the crew tried to escape from the ship and lowered the ship's boat into the sea as though they meant to lay out anchors from the bows, Paul said to the centurion and his men, 'Unless those men stay on board, you cannot hope to be saved.' So the soldiers cut the boat's ropes and let it drop away" (Acts 27:27-32).

The first detail we have to consider in this paragraph is the amount of time that the ship took to drift from Gavdos to *Melítē*, a total of fourteen days. Smith makes his calculation and arrives at the following conclusion:

> "The next point to be ascertained is, how far would she have driven from Cauda about midnight 'when the fourteenth night was come.' The knowledge of this depends upon the rate of drift and the time consumed. The result which the calculation founded upon these data gives us is so very striking, that I feel called upon to state the elements on which it is founded at some length."[64]

Smith consulted two expert sailors of the Levant, Captain W. McLean and Captain Graves, who stated that a ship during ancient times could drift according to the force of this gale for about 40 miles in 24 hours (McLean), or about 33 miles in 24 hours (Graves). Smith calculated the mean of these extremes and arrived at 36.5 miles in 24 hours. He states that the distance from Cauda to the point of Koura or Qawra at the tip of St. Paul's Bay, where he supposes that the sailors became aware that land was nearing, is 476.6 miles (766 kilometres), which would amount to a total of 13 days, 1 hour and 21 minutes. "The coincidence of the actual bearing of St. Paul's Bay from Clauda, and the direction in which a ship must have driven in order to avoid the Syrtis, is, if possible, still more striking than that of the time actually consumed, and the calculated time."[65]

---

[64] J. Smith (1880), 84.
[65] J. Smith (1880), 86.

The stretch of sea lying between Gavdos and Malta is called "Adriatic", or "Adria". We have already seen the detailed discussion that the name introduced in the interpretations of both Đurđević and Ciantar, who refer to authors of antiquity regarding the division between the "Adriatic Gulf" (modern Adriatic Sea) and the "Sea of Adria", extending outwards to the Ionian Sea or *Mare Siculum*. From the detailed analysis of Smith, we have logically to exclude the Adriatic understood as the sea extending inwards from the Straits of Otranto and opt for the wide stretch of sea extending from Crete westwards towards Sicily and Malta. It is only in this section, which includes the deepest basin in the Mediterranean and the subsequent rift of the African plate at the Malta Escarpment, that we can possibly analyse the phenomenon of the ENE wind that made the ship drift WNW towards Malta, and not NNW towards Mljet.

The fact that the sailors sensed that land was approaching is a result of their initial fears of being shipwrecked on the Syrtis Banks. The *Syrtis Maior* Banks in Libya, extending from Cyrenaica to Sidra (Sirte), in the Gulf of Syrte, were notoriously dangerous for shipping in ancient times because of the treacherous sand shoals and sea currents. As we have seen, had the ship been left at the mercy of the sea currents and waves, and especially at the mercy of the strong ENE gale, she would have drifted forward before the storm and would have foundered precisely on the Syrtis Banks. Given that the sailors had done all they could to avoid such a catastrophe, the ship was controlled in such a way that she drifted sideways at an angle, in the direction that the anti-cyclonic system was taking, namely, due WNW, just some degrees north of west, towards Tunisia. That was the only possible direction of the gale originating in southern Crete. Any interpretation of a sudden change of the wind in a NNW direction towards the Adriatic and hence towards Mljet, has to be excluded.

How did the sailors know that land was approaching? It was still night and they could not possibly have seen the shoreline. Even if it were possible to see land, Malta does not have any high mountains that can be seen from far out at sea, and its northern coast is low-lying, although on clear days it can be visible from as far out as 15-20 kilometres distance. According to Smith:

> "If we assume that Saint Paul's Bay, in Malta, is the actual scene of the shipwreck, we can have no difficulty in explaining what these indications must have been. No ship can enter it from the east without passing within a quarter of a mile of the point of Koura; but, before reaching it, the land is too low, and too far from the track of a ship driven from the eastward, to be seen on a dark night. When she does come within this distance, it is impossible to avoid observing the breakers; for, with the north-easterly gales, the sea breaks upon it with such violence."[66]

[66] J. Smith (1880), 79.

The place to which Smith refers is Qawra point, where a low, rocky promontory marks, to this very day, the entrance to Salina Bay on one side, and to Saint Paul's Bay on the other. It is truly a place "where two seas meet", although we can find other places fitting the same description in Malta. It is battered on the outer flank by the NW gales, which are fairly common in winter, but it is also open to the ENE gales, and looks directly ahead of any ship arriving to Malta on a straight course from the east. The sailors could very well have been aware that waves were crashing against a rocky shore on the port side of the ship, when they were passing close to Salina Bay and entering Saint Paul's Bay, according to the interpretation given by Smith.

> "Just before daybreak, Paul urged them all to have something to eat. 'For fourteen days', he said, 'you have been in suspense, going hungry and eating nothing. I urge you to have something to eat; your safety depends on it. Not a hair of any of your heads will be lost.' With these words he took some bread, gave thanks to God in view of them all, broke it and began to eat. They all plucked up courage and took something to eat themselves. In all we were two hundred and seventy-six souls on board that ship. When they had eaten what they wanted, they lightened the ship by throwing the corn overboard into the sea" (Acts 27:33-38).

The reason why the sailors and passengers on the ship were famished was simple. They were so weary of keeping everything under control on the ship, which was probably taking in water and was in danger of foundering because of the strength of the waves, that they scarcely had any time to eat, and obviously were unable to cook or prepare any food. Some biblical commentators have suggested a "Eucharistic" style in this narrative, because of the actions of Paul ("he took some bread, gave thanks to God in view of them all, broke it and began to eat"). Seemingly this was not Luke's intention or interpretation of the fact, but since Paul was a Jew, he obviously took food by following the typical Jewish rites of blessing and breaking the bread, which is very similar to the Eucharistic actions of Jesus and the early Christians.[67]

---

[67] L.T. JOHNSON (1992) 455: "The fourfold action of taking (*labōn*), giving thanks (*eucharístēsen*), breaking (*klásas*) and beginning to eat (*ērxato esthíein*) need not refer to the Eucharist, since all Jewish meals involved the saying of blessings; but the sequence is sufficiently allusive to point the reader back to earlier passages where the Eucharistic gestures seem deliberately to be invoked (see Luke 6:4; 9:16; 22:19; 24:30). The addition of 'having given also to us' in the Western Text makes the allusion even stronger. The real point of the gesture, however, is found in the phrase *enōpion pántōn* ('in front of them all'): Paul is presenting an example for them, one which in fact they imitate (see also Luke 24:43)." J. GILL, http://www/studylight.org/commentaries/gebh/acts-27.html (accessed 8 September 2017): "A piece of bread, of common bread, into his hands; for this could never be the Eucharist, or Lord's supper, which the apostle now celebrated, as some have suggested, but such sort of bread that seafaring men commonly eat: mention is before made of 'meat' or 'food', which the apostle entreated them to take, which includes every sort of sea provisions they had with them; and which, with the ancients, were

The shipwreck

"When day came, they did not recognise the land, but they could make out a bay with a beach; they planned to run the ship aground on this if they could. They slipped the anchors and let them fall into the sea, and at the same time loosened the lashings of the rudders; then, hoisting the foresail to the wind, they headed for the beach. But the cross-currents carried them into a shoal and the vessel ran aground. The bows were wedged in and stuck fast, while the stern began to break up with the pounding of the waves. The soldiers planned to kill the prisoners for fear that any should swim off and escape. But the centurion was determined to bring Paul safely through and would not let them carry out their plan. He gave orders that those who could swim should jump overboard first and so get ashore, and the rest follow either on planks or on pieces of wreckage. In this way it happened that all came safe and sound to land" (Acts 27:39-44).

39 Ὅτε δὲ ἡμέρα ἐγένετο, τὴν γῆν οὐκ ἐπεγίνωσκον, κόλπον δέ τινα κατενόουν ἔχοντα
αἰγιαλὸν εἰς ὃν ἐβουλεύοντο εἰ δύναιντο ἐξῶσαι τὸ πλοῖον. 40 καὶ τὰς ἀγκύρας περιελόντες
εἴων εἰς τὴν θάλασσαν, ἅμα ἀνέντες τὰς ζευκτηρίας τῶν πηδαλίων καὶ ἐπάραντες τὸν
ἀρτέμωνα τῇ πνεούσῃ κατεῖχον εἰς τὸν αἰγιαλόν. 41 περιπεσόντες δὲ εἰς τόπον διθάλασσον
ἐπέκειλαν τὴν ναῦν καὶ ἡ μὲν πρῷρα ἐρείσασα ἔμεινεν ἀσάλευτος, ἡ δὲ πρύμνα ἐλύετο
ὑπὸ τῆς βίας [τῶν κυμάτων]. 42 Τῶν δὲ στρατιωτῶν βουλὴ ἐγένετο ἵνα τοὺς δεσμώτας
ἀποκτείνωσιν, μή τις ἐκκολυμβήσας διαφύγῃ. 43 ὁ δὲ ἑκατοντάρχης βουλόμενος διασῶσαι
τὸν Παῦλον ἐκώλυσεν αὐτοὺς τοῦ βουλήματος, ἐκέλευσέν τε τοὺς δυναμένους κολυμβᾶν
ἀπορίψαντας πρώτους ἐπὶ τὴν γῆν ἐξιέναι 44 καὶ τοὺς λοιποὺς οὓς μὲν ἐπὶ σανίσιν, οὓς δὲ
ἐπί τινων τῶν ἀπὸ τοῦ πλοίου. καὶ οὕτως ἐγένετο πάντας διασωθῆναι ἐπὶ τὴν γῆν.

The account of the shipwreck contains many interesting details that could provide clues as to the actual place where it all happened. Unfortunately, attempts to identify the exact place of the shipwreck on Malta have not yielded results which are entirely satisfactory. Our attempt, therefore, will be just another presentation of the various possibilities that the Maltese coast offers, which maybe can never be finally resolved because of lack of archaeological or documentary evidence.

---

usually the following: it is certain they used to carry bread corn along with them, either crude, or ground, or baked; the former when they went long voyages, the last when shorter ones; and it is plain that they had wheat in this ship, which after they had eaten they cast out, Acts 27:38, and corn ground, or meal, they had used to eat moistened with water, and sometimes with oil, and sometimes with oil and wine; and they had a sort of food they called *maza* which was made of meat and milk; likewise they used to carry onions and garlic, which the rowers usually ate, and were thought to be good against change of places and water; and they were wont to make a sort of soup of cheese, onions and eggs, which the Greeks call *myttōtós*, and the Latins *mosetum*; and they had also bread which was of a red colour, being hard baked and scorched in the oven, yea it was *biscoctus*, twice baked; as our modern sea biscuit is, and which has its name from hence, and which for long voyages is four times baked, and prepared six months before the voyage is entered on; and such sort of red bread or biscuit very probably was this, which the apostle now took into his hands." Cfr. A.M. Buscemi (1997) 237.

Luke first states that "when day came they could not recognise the land." This affirmation is taken by Đurđević to mean that the island in question could not possibly have been Malta, since Malta has excellent harbours, which are well known by seamen, whereas Mljet lies off the beaten track. However, Đurđević does not admit that the fact that the sailors could not recognise the land depended on various factors. First of all, Malta is not a mountainous island, contrary to Mljet which is clearly visible with its craggy peaks covered with Mediterranean pines and lush vegetation. Malta is rather barren[68] and low-lying, at least on its northern flanks, and it arrives at 300 metres above sea-level on the cliffs of the southwest coast. Secondly, while it is true that Malta has excellent harbours, which were well-known to seafarers ever since the times of the Phoenicians, it was probable that the sailors could have been acquainted with the large harbours used by Roman ships, namely Marsaxlokk Bay, the Grand Harbour, and Marsamxett Harbour. Saint Paul's Bay was also a large harbour and could be used for anchoring ships, but it lay further north and was definitely more open to the ravaging effects of an ENE gale. It certainly was not a preferred harbour for anchoring ships in winter and could only have been chosen because of a situation of emergency.

The sailors "could make out a bay with a beach." This is one of the few indications that Luke gives us regarding the "bay" in which the sailors tried to run the ship aground in order to be able to make safely to shore. The indication is not very clear and it is truly difficult to come to any clear-cut conclusion as to the bay to which Luke is referring.[69] We shall try to make conjectures with our knowledge of the Maltese coast.

A look at the map of Malta shows that the island has a long coastline facing directly NE from *Aħrax Point* in *Mellieħa* to *Żonqor Point* at *Wied il-Għajn*. Then the coast turns south and faces E from *Żonqor Point* to *Delimara Peninsula* and *Marsaxlokk Bay*, which is open to the SE. In practice, we are dealing with half of the coast of Malta. The rest of the coast looks SW, W and NW, and lies beyond the scope of our analysis.

---

68 Was Malta barren in Roman times? Maybe not. The Arabs chopped off many of the trees on the island.

69 I am, however, indebted to Profs Horatio Vella for his expert advice on the matter. According to him, a bay with a beach facing the ENE wind fits in perfectly with the position of Saint Paul's Bay. Quintinus tells us that the name of the bay had been given to it from very ancient times (*vetusissime*). Vella (1980), 45: "In this way the Maltese sailors include Paul in the history of their land: above all they point at and venerate his footsteps in many places. The shore of that place, which is between two seas (*loci illius bimaris*), can actually be visited (according to Ptolemy it is called *hersonesos*, as indeed it is); it has from very ancient times (*vetusissime*) derived its name from Paul in as much as it is the site of the shipwreck. There is a small chapel in stone, not the least venerated in the island."

If we try to pinpoint the places on this stretch of coast, which have "a bay with a beach", going from north to south, we would first encounter Malta's largest bay, namely *Mellieħa Bay*, which faces directly NE. It is clearly visible from a good distance out at sea and has a sandy beach and also a shoal which lies just about 3 metres below sea level at the centre of the bay within swimming distance to the beach. One also has to add an interesting feature, namely, a large shoal known as *Is-Sikka l-Bajda*, which lies out of the *Aħrax Cliffs*, or *Rdum l-Aħmar* in a NE direction. It lies some 2.5 kilometres offshore and has an average depth of 15 metres. Although tectonic forces could have played a part in subsidence during geological times, it is difficult to accept that it was anywhere close to sea level when Paul was shipwrecked, and even so, it lies too far out to offer any hope of survival for 276 shipwrecked souls in a force 8 ENE gale.

The next large bay is *Saint Paul's Bay*, which is considered to be the traditional place of the shipwreck. It also looks due NE. We shall describe this bay in greater detail. Here let it suffice to say that there are various parts of the bay that could fit Luke's description. It is a "bay with a beach", having other inlets on both sides, particularly *Mistra Bay*, also having a small beach, the islet of *Selmunett* at the northwest tip, considered as one of the traditional spots of the shipwreck, as well as *Qawra Point* at the opposite end. Both these rocky features have all the appearance of a "place where two seas meet." On the eastern shore of the bay one also finds the rocks known as *Tal-Għażżenin*. Some distance away there is a shoal (1.5 metres below sea level). This is the place where, since ancient times, the Maltese revered the welcoming of Paul and his companions. It is marked by the church of *San Pawl tal-Ħġejjeġ*. Wigacourt's Tower stands further away, close to the *Tal-Għażżenin* rocks. Some distance away from the islet of *Selmunett*, roughly at the centre of the bay, is a shoal called in Maltese *Is-Sikka ta' San Pawl* (Saint Paul's Shoal), but it lies at about 11.6 metres below sea level.[70]

On the other side of *Qawra Point* is *Salina Bay*. Nowadays it looks like a shallow bay with a narrow inlet filled with salt-pans and fed by fresh water when the rains come, descending from the longest *wadi* in Malta, known by various names at various stages, *Wied Liemu, Wied il-Fiddien, Wied il-Qlejgħa (Chadwick Lakes), Wied il-Għasel* and the ex-marshland of *Burmarrad*. This bay also looks NE and there were no salt pans when Paul was shipwrecked, so it could very well have had a beach and a creek clearly visible from some distance out at sea.

---

[70] The idea of a shoal referred to the place of the shipwreck does not correspond to the Greek term *dithálassos*. This would refer to a piece of land having the sea on both parts (for example, a stretch of low-lying land jutting out into the sea). So, it is not a shoal. The translation in "ran aground into a shoal" (Maltese, "ħbatna ma' sikka") is therefore incorrect.

Going further down along the coast one encounters a rocky shoal known as *Il-Blata tal-Għallis*. Most of it is above sea level and is quite close to land, in such a way that, on calm days, one can practically wade to it from the coast. Although it could be treacherous for shipping, it is too close to land to have been the place of the shipwreck, even though it is a place of cross-currents when it is buffeted by waves coming from the NW or the NE. Some distance further one encounters the *Qala San Marku Bay*, a small bay with a beach, but this faces the NW and is not directly visible to a ship coming from an ENE direction. Outside the eastern flank of the *Qala San Marku peninsula* is a shoal, known by the same name, facing E. It lies in the open sea, although it is not far away from the coast.

Another interesting place further down the coast is *Il-Bajja ta' San Ġorġ* and *Il-Qaliet*, looking also NE, and having a headland, *Il-Ponta tad-Dragunara* with shoals ranging from 5.6 to 7.6 metres below sea level. It is a small and narrow bay, but it does have a beach and is clearly visible for a ship approaching the island diagonally at an ENE direction. Close by is also *Il-Bajja ta' San Ġiljan*, again another small bay with a beach, looking ENE.

At this point one encounters the two main harbours of Malta, namely *Marsamxett Harbour* and *Grand Harbour*, with their famous natural creeks and peninsulas, and the natural divide of the peninsula of *Mount Xiberras*, known also in antiquity as *Xagħret Mewwija*, where the city of Valletta was built. It is not necessary to enter into a detailed description of the two harbours, since they were well known in antiquity and were safe havens for ships plying the central Mediterranean. Both harbours are open to the ENE gales, and indeed the *Grigal* gales are a spectacular site at their entrances to this very day. Given that the sailors did not recognise the land, it is highly improbable that they were the site of the shipwreck.

The coastline from *Ricasoli Point* to *Żonqor Point*, passing through *Ix-Xgħajra ta'Ħaż-Żabbar*, is a fairly straight and rocky shore, with no bays or beaches worthy of note. At *Żonqor Point* the coast turns abruptly south, facing directly E. The first bay with a beach is that of *Wied il-Għajn*, or *Marsaskala*, between *Żonqor Point* and *It-Torri ta' San Tumas*. This bay looks E, but the beach is not directly visible since inland the coast curves facing NE.

Of greater interest to our study is the *Bajja ta' San Tumas*, a bay with a beach, which faces directly E towards Crete. Indeed, it could be one of the first bays that a ship coming from the ENE would see on the coast of Malta. It is enclosed between a small peninsula where the *Torri ta' San Tumas* is situated, and a more prominent whitish and chalky peninsula known as *Il-Munxar*. This peninsula is quite interesting, since it ends in a point overlooking white cliffs near *Il-Ħofra l-Kbira*. If one looks at a satellite image of this headland, one notices that it extends underwater for quite a considerable distance. It forms a sandy shoal, which is just 1.2 metres below sea level. The shoal is a clear sign of intense weathering of the friable chalky limestone, and one has the impression that two millennia ago the headland would have extended far out at sea. Indeed, the view from the outer sea would be that of a bay with a beach. In the case of an ENE gale, the waves would crash against *Il-Munxar* headland with intense fury, creating many cross-currents and giving the idea of a place between two seas. I personally have gone to check out how the sea would look on a stormy day in which the *Grigal* gale blows. The sight was truly spectacular. The cross-currents were evident and they would divide into two directions. Indeed, the shoal fits in perfectly with what Luke states in the Acts, namely, that it was a place where two seas meet, outside a bay with a beach. I wondered whether this could have been the actual place of the shipwreck, rather than Saint Paul's Bay. It is the first land one sights when coming from the direction of Crete. Having said this, however, one has to remember that the ship came from Crete in a swerve, from a SW direction, and therefore would not have necessarily been thrown in this bay but could proceed along the NE coast towards Saint Paul's Bay. There are some who hold that this was the place of the shipwreck because ancient Roman anchors have been found embedded in the shoal. However, the same thing can be stated regarding other shoals we have mentioned. What struck me most, however, was the destructive force of the waves. Although the place fits in perfectly with Luke's narration, if a ship got stuck on the shoal in the fury of a *Grigal* storm, it would have been torn in pieces. What is more improbable is the possibility to save oneself by swimming inland from that point. Although the water is not deep, the sheer force of the waves and storm surge would make it difficult to swim to safety. When I witnessed the sight of the waves from above the cliff I wondered whether there would have been any survivors had Paul and his companions been shipwrecked on the *Muxar* shoal.

The link with Saint Paul in this part of the coast is not too evident, but it exists. For one thing, there is a tiny semi-dilapidated church some metres further inland from *Il-Munxar Point*, at *Xrobb l-Għaġin*.[71] The church is not built upon early Christian remains, but it is a sign that somehow the event of the shipwreck has historically also been linked to this section of the island. Another important detail to remember is that, some distance away, lie the archaeological remains of *Tas-Silġ*. On this spot, there are the remains of the Temple dedicated to the Phoenician goddess Astarte (equivalent to the Roman Juno, *Fanum Iunonis*), built around 700 B.C. upon the remains of one or more megalithic temples from the Tarxien phase

[71] This church is dedicated to the Shipwreck of Saint Paul. It was originally built in 1751 during the Grand Mastership of Emanuel Pinto de Fonseca, and was restored in 1831. It lies adjacent to *It-Torri ta' Bettina*, in a plot of land which is private property. The church and tower are easily visible from the sea and could very well have been built in support of the opinion that the Apostle was shipwrecked on this section of the coast. The naming of this church after Saint Paul is counterbalanced by the naming of another church after Saint Luke on the other side of Marsaxlokk Bay, near Bengħisa.

(3000 B.C.) and destined to become a Byzantine monastery and basilica (400-600 A.D.).[72] The location of *Tas-Silġ*, high on the promontory of *Delimara* between *Marsaxlokk* and *Il-Munxar*, throws light upon the importance of this place which was well-known to sea-farers ever since Phoenician and Punic times.[73]

The *Delimara Peninsula* offers other bays, namely, *Il-Ħofra l-Kbira, Il-Ħofra ż-Żgħira* and *Saint Peter's Pool*. Although they are picturesque bays, they are made up rather of friable whitish rocks more than sand, and do not have proper beaches. The last large and important bay is *Marsaxlokk Harbour*, which is nowadays sadly ruined by the concrete breakwater and Malta Freeport on one side and by the Power Station and LNG Tanker on the other. In the pristine beauty of the surroundings, it used to be a beautiful fishing harbour, and was well known to Phoenician traders, since it looks SE and is big enough to be seen from far out at sea for any vessel coming from the direction of the Eastern Mediterranean. Had Paul's ship made *Marsaxlokk*, the author of Acts would not have stated that the sailors could not recognise the land. This is the last possible bay with a beach on this section of Malta. From *Bengħisa* the coast turns west, facing SW and is made up of cliffs and craggy rocks, with few inlets. The bays and beaches further north look towards W or NW and are therefore outside the scope of our analysis.

This description of the coast of Malta which faces NE, ENE and E is a sign of the great difficulty to individuate the place of the shipwreck. We shall continue to speak about the place indicated by J. Smith as corresponding more closely to the probable spot, namely Saint Paul's Bay, the traditional place of the shipwreck of the Apostle.[74]

According to Smith's calculations the bearings and position of Saint Paul's Bay fit in perfectly with Luke's narrative. The ship was approaching Malta from an ENE direction. It was still dark and the sailors had an inkling that land was approaching. Any ship which approaches Saint Paul's Bay from the ENE must necessarily enter it by passing close to the rocky headland of *Qawra* between Saint Paul's Bay and Salina Bay. As Smith has aptly noted, the sound of the breakers on these rocks was a warning sign to the sailors. That is why they made soundings and found 20 and then 15 fathoms of depth. In order to arrest the ship's movements, the sailors dropped anchors from the stern, in such a way as to keep it fairly stable in its position. The sea floor at Saint Paul's Bay is full of clay and mud, and it would

---

72 H.C.R. VELLA (1982), 274-275: "Recent excavations at Tas-Silġ near Delimara by the Missione Archeologica Italiana a Malta have shown that the remains of a temple on top of that hill actually belonged to the temple of Juno. Quintinus describes these remains as of stupendous height and width and covering a very wide space, in that part of the island which the Maltese call Marsaxlokk."

73 M. BUHAGIAR (1996), 1-41; D.H. TRUMP (2002), 138-139; A. BONANNO (2005), 271-272; E. WATTS-PLUMPKIN (2013): world.archaeology.com (accessed 8 September 2017).

74 J. SMITH (1880), 88-107.

hold an anchor in position fairly successfully even in the teeth of an ENE gale. In the meantime, the sailors prayed for daylight.

As soon as they could make out land, the sailors could not recognise it. It was a section of the coast of Malta that they had never seen. On their left was the rocky headland of *Qawra*. Further inland there was the low-lying shore of the bay ending in a beach with a bay. Straight ahead, on the other side of the bay, they could make out a rocky shore. They certainly had *Mistra Bay* ahead of them, although it is not perfectly aligned to the NE. However, all around the area were rocks, and between *Mistra* and the islet of *Selmunett* there are cliffs. To run a ship aground on that side of the bay would have spelt disaster. According to Smith, they had just one option, namely to try to make it to a low-lying section of the coast known as *Blata l-Bajda* just some metres away from the islet of *Selmunett*. At this point there is a narrow channel, which is only 1.2 metres deep. During an ENE gale, it does provide a relatively calmer area, since it is more open to the NW gales. Maybe the sailors had no way of knowing that the water was so shallow, and that the ship would end up wedged on the soft rocky and sandy bottom of the channel. This was, always according to Smith, the τόπον διθάλασσον, the place "where two seas meet." It indeed fits in perfectly with Luke's description, although, as we shall now see, it does not solve the problem entirely. Tradition has ascribed to this spot the honour of having been the place of Paul's shipwreck, but it is fairly recent.[75]

After describing the sailing techniques adopted by the sailors to make for land, including the loosing the lashes of the rudders and the hoisting of the foresail, or artemon, Smith minutely describes the actual shipwreck, and seems to indicate this

---

[75] The island of *Selmunett*, surmounted by the statue of Saint Paul, commemorates the location of the shipwreck. It is an islet of just 0.1 km^2, and geologically is the continuation of the headland of *Selmun*, which used to be the property of the *Salomone* family (hence the name in Maltese) after 1575. High up on the *Selmun* headland stands the palace of Selmun, built during the 18th century by the charity *Monte della Redenzione degli Schiavi*, founded by Grand Master Alof de Wignacourt in 1607. The islet is made up of two parts, the higher and larger section close to the headland, and another small rock, joined to it by an isthmus, called *Quartz Island* (hence the improper plural Saint Paul's Islands, or *Il-Gżejjer ta' San Pawl* in Maltese). In 1649, Grand Master Jean Paul Lascaris built a watch tower on the islet, and it became property of the Order of Saint John. The tower sadly lies in ruins, and for some decades, until 1930, it was inhabited by a Maltese farmer. The statue of Saint Paul, which stands prominently on a stone pedestal, was sculptured in 1844 by Sigismondo and Salvatore Dimech. It was blessed and inaugurated on 21 September 1845. It has been ravaged by erosion during the years, but was restored in 1966 and 2015. Pope John Paul II was taken close to the islet by catamaran in 1990. Celebrations were held on the islet to mark the 1900 years of the shipwreck of Saint Paul in 1960, as well as during the special year dedicated to Saint Paul in 2008. However, neither Pope John Paul II nor Pope Benedict XVI set foot on the islet of *Selmunett*, although John Paul II did stop close by when a fibreglass statue of Christ was submerged in the vicinity of the islet. It has since been moved to another place close to Qawra point.

spot on the western side of the bay as the place of the shipwreck, contrary to the more ancient tradition handed down by Quintinus, which places it on the opposite shore where the church of Saint Paul was built:

> "The ship must have been driven to the west side of the bay, which is rocky, but has two creeks. One of these, Mestara (Mistra) Valley, has a shore. I am, however, inclined to think that the point of appulse was in the creek, which has no longer a sandy beach, but which must have had one formerly, although now worn away by the wasting action of the sea; it is near the spot marked in the chart of St. Pauls' Bay, as the traditional scene of the wreck. My chief reason for supposing that it was hereabouts that the ship was run ashore is its proximity to what St. Luke calls 'a place of two seas' (τόπον διθάλασσον), or, as our authorised version renders it by a happy conjecture, 'a place where two seas meet.' From the entrance of the bay, where the ship must have been anchored, they could not possibly have suspected that at the bottom of it there should be a communication with the sea outside; this unexpected circumstance naturally attracted the attention of the author, and served to mark the spot where the ship was wrecked. Selmoon (Selmun) Island, which separates the bay from the sea on the outside, is formed by a long rocky ridge, separated from the main land by a channel of not more than a hundred yards in breadth. Near this channel, which a glance at the chart will show must be where a ship from the eastward would be driven, they ran the ship ashore; the fore part stuck fast and remained entire, but the stern was dashed to pieces by the force of the waves. This is a remarkable circumstance, which, but for the peculiar nature of the bottom of St. Paul's Bay, it would be difficult to account for."[76]

The interpretation given by Smith is the result of an expert analysis of the meteorological elements, coupled with the experience of seamanship. It does, however, leave us with a set of unanswered questions. Why is it that the local tradition of the location of Paul's shipwreck near *Selmunett* is so fairly recent, when compared to the more ancient tradition locating the shipwreck on the opposite shore, near the church of *San Pawl tal-Ħġejjeġ*? Even if we accept Smith's thesis, how could the islanders have welcomed the survivors in such a remote area of the coast? Until this very day, the *Selmun* headland is still luckily untouched by human development. Was it more natural for the indigenous inhabitants of *Melítē* to welcome the company of shipwrecked souls on the opposite shore, which at the time was within visible distance of inhabited areas, such as the *Wardija* hills or *Burmarrad*, where the Roman remains of *San Pawl Milqi* stand? All in all, we can state that, until fairly recent times, the area of Malta standing north of the Great Fault, running from the *Madliena Tower* at *Baħar iċ-Ċagħaq* to *Fomm ir-Riħ Bay*, was rather uninhabited. All these questions are, unfortunately, difficult to answer and resolve in a satisfactory way. All we can say is that, given the expert analysis of J. Smith which we have outlined, the indication of an area within Saint Paul's Bay as the more probable location of the shipwreck is acceptable, as long as we do not find further proofs to the contrary.

---

[76] J. Smith (1880), 102-103.

Concluding remarks

Many have tried to come to terms with Luke's description of Paul's shipwreck in Acts with the help of historical documentation, archaeological evidence, and modern knowhow of meteorological phenomena and shipping techniques. The result has been a renewed interest in locating the exact spot where Paul was shipwrecked in Malta. In our analysis, we might have been too limited in our description, since we based many of our arguments on the publication of J. Smith, which is nearly two centuries old. However, the study of these phenomena linked with the "Maltese" tradition of Paul's shipwreck, has not yet found a definite solution, and Smith's work still remains one among the best of its kind. Unfortunately, we have assisted at many new theories advanced with an aim of enhancing Malta's popularity as a centre for "religious tourism", but which are lacking in scientific analysis.

It has not been our aim to provide a solution to the various questions that we ourselves have proposed. What is clear, however, is that Luke's description of the gale and shipwreck is rich in details, but not rich enough to arrive at any hard and fast conclusion. Luke's aim was not that of simply providing an account of an epic sea voyage, but rather that of showing how the Gospel arrived "to earth's remotest end" (Acts 1:8) through the ministry of the Apostle Paul.[77] Many factors do, however, point to the right direction. Given the space of two millennia, with the inevitable geological and tectonic changes that might have occurred along the coast of Malta, we still have the luck of observing the meteorological phenomena that brought Paul to our shores. One thing is certainly clear, and Smith proves it, namely, that the ENE gale blowing from Crete could only have carried the ship towards Malta. Any other interpretations, which must be respectfully considered, including the *Cephalonia* and *Mljet* theories, are still in need of a thorough meteorological analysis of the phenomena described by Luke, in order to understand how the gale could have possibly carried the ship northwards into the Adriatic.

One last theme is also important to analyse, namely, the "Pauline" cult in Malta and the various places linked with the presence of the Apostle. Indeed, it is difficult, also in this regard, to arrive at any clear-cut statement when one takes into consideration that the earliest Christian places of cult and memories on the Maltese archipelago go back at the earliest to the 4th century, namely to the late Roman domination of the islands. What occurred during apostolic times is still shrouded in mystery, except for the fact that Paul did stay on *Melítē* for three months, and that his evangelising ministry could not possibly have been halted by the fact that Malta was pagan and Roman religion honoured emperors as gods. Therefore Paul's visit did produce the seeds of what we can call an "apostolic Church" in Malta.

---

[77] L.T. Johnson (1992), 444-467.

Chapter 5

The cult of Saint Paul on the Island of Malta

The Acts of the Apostles speak about the presence of Saint Paul on *Melítē* during the winter months of A.D. 60-61, stating that he left *Melítē* "at the end of three months" (Acts 28:11). The episode of the shipwreck on *Melítē* stops short of giving us a detailed analysis of the events during this period of time. It describes in some detail what happened as soon as the survivors landed on the island, how they were welcomed by Publius, how Paul cured Publius' father from dysentery as well as the other islanders, and how the same natives honoured the guests by providing them with many provisions before they set sail for Italy. It is clear that Luke's intention is that of skimming over Paul's stay on the island, which he deems as not highly relevant in his plan, namely, that of making Paul arrive in Rome in order to render witness to Christ in the capital of the Roman empire. Malta was just a stop-over during this eventful journey.

Having said this, it is difficult to imagine that Paul was standing idle during three whole months, even though he was marooned on a small island in the centre of the Mediterranean. Local Maltese traditions abound with references to the presence and apostolic ministry of Paul. As we have seen, we are unfortunate that there is hardly any documentary evidence of a Christian presence on the island during the first centuries of Christianity, except for the episode of Paul's visit in Acts. Even so, traditions are not born out of pure imagination, and one can try to discover the grain of truth underlying them, even with the help of archaeological evidence.

What we intend to do in this last chapter of our analysis is that of first continuing to see what Luke has to say in the narrative of Acts 28:1-11, and then to mention the various traditions and places linked with the presence of Saint Paul in Malta. We do not intend to question their historical validity, but rather to link them to the narrative of the Acts and see how popular beliefs and devotions in Malta were born out of a continuous link with the undisputed fact that the apostle Paul had set foot on the island. At this stage, it is obviously irrelevant to continue to underline the thesis of an alternative place linked with the shipwreck of Saint Paul, such as the island of Mljet, and rather to concentrate on the more concrete possibility that the island of *Melítē* mentioned in Acts 28:1 is none other than Malta.

Paul on the island of Malta according to Acts 28:1-11

“[1] Once we had come safely through, we discovered that the island was called Malta. [2] The inhabitants treated us with unusual kindness. They made us all welcome by lighting a huge fire because it had started to rain and the weather was cold. [3] Paul had collected a bundle of sticks and was putting them on the fire when a viper brought out by the heat attached itself to his hand. [4] When the inhabitants saw the creature hanging from his hand, they said to one another, ‘That man must be a murderer; he may have escaped the sea, but divine justice would not let him live.’ [5] However, he shook the creature off into the fire and came to no harm, [6] although they were expecting him at any moment to swell up or drop dead on the spot. After they had waited a long time without seeing anything out of the ordinary happen to him, they changed their minds and began to say he was a god. [7] In that neighbourhood there were estates belonging to the chief man of the island, whose name was Publius. He received us and entertained us hospitably for three days. [8] It happened that Publius’ father was in bed, suffering from fever and dysentery. Paul went in to see him, and after a prayer, he laid his hands on the man and healed him. [9] When this happened, the other sick people on the island also came and were cured; [10] they honoured us with many marks of respect, and when we sailed they put on board the provisions we needed. [11] At the end of three months we set sail in a ship that had wintered in the island; she came from Alexandria and her figurehead was the Twins.”

[1] Καὶ διασωθέντες τότε ἐπέγνωμεν ὅτι Μελίτη ἡ νῆσος καλεῖται. [2] οἵ τε βάρβαροι παρεῖχον οὐ τὴν τυχοῦσαν φιλανθρωπίαν ἡμῖν, ἅψαντες γὰρ πυρὰν προσελάβοντο πάντας ἡμᾶς διὰ τὸν ὑετὸν τὸν ἐφεστῶτα καὶ διὰ τὸ ψῦχος. [3] συστρέψαντος δὲ τοῦ Παύλου φρυγάνων τι πλῆθος καὶ ἐπιθέντος ἐπὶ τὴν πυράν, ἔχιδνα ἀπὸ τῆς θέρμης ἐξελθοῦσα καθῆψε τῆς χειρὸς αὐτοῦ. [4] ὡς δὲ εἶδον οἱ βάρβαροι κρεμάμενον τὸ θηρίον ἐκ τῆς χειρὸς αὐτοῦ, πρὸς ἀλλήλους ἔλεγον. Πάντως φονεύς ἐστιν ὁ ἄνθρωπος οὗτος ὃν διασωθέντα ἐκ τῆς θαλάσσης ἡ δίκη ζῆν οὐκ εἴασεν. [5] ὁ μὲν οὖν ἀποτινάξας τὸ θηρίον εἰς τὸ πῦρ ἔπαθεν οὐδὲν κακόν. [6] οἱ δὲ προσεδόκων αὐτὸν μέλλειν πίμπρασθαι ἢ καταπίπτειν ἄφνω νεκρόν. ἐπὶ πολὺ δὲ αὐτῶν προσδοκώντων καὶ θεωρούντων μηδὲν ἄτοπον εἰς αὐτὸν γινόμενον, μεταβαλόμενοι ἔλεγον αὐτὸν εἶναι θεόν. [7] Ἐν δὲ τοῖς περὶ τὸν τόπον ἐκεῖνον ὑπῆρχεν χωρία τῷ πρώτῳ τῆς νήσου ὀνόματι Ποπλίῳ, ὃς ἀναδεξάμενος ἡμᾶς τρεῖς ἡμέρας φιλοφρόνως ἐξένισεν. [8] ἐγένετο δὲ τὸν πατέρα τοῦ Ποπλίου πυρετοῖς καὶ δυσεντερίῳ συνεχόμενον κατακεῖσθαι, πρὸς ὃν ὁ Παῦλος εἰσελθὼν καὶ προσευξάμενος ἐπιθεὶς τὰς χεῖρας αὐτῷ ἰάσατο αὐτόν. [9] τούτου δὲ γενομένου καὶ οἱ λοιποὶ οἱ ἐν τῇ νήσῳ ἔχοντες ἀσθενείας προσήρχοντο καὶ ἐθεραπεύοντο, [10] οἳ καὶ πολλαῖς τιμαῖς ἐτίμησαν ἡμᾶς καὶ ἀναγομένοις ἐπέθεντο τὰ πρὸς τὰς χρείας. [11] Μετὰ δὲ τρεῖς μῆνας ἀνήχθημεν ἐν πλοίῳ παρακεχειμακότι ἐν τῇ νήσῳ Ἀλεξανδρίνῳ, παρασήμῳ Διοσκούροις.

The name of the island, *Melítē* (Μελίτη) became evident to the survivors only after they had landed safely. This is another proof that they had totally lost their bearings. Malta was not off the beaten track of Mediterranean shipping. It had been colonised by the Phoenicians precisely as a safe haven (the Phoenician name *Maleth*, which is considered to have given origin to the Greek name *Melítē* and to the Roman *Melita*, to be subsequently developed into the Arabic name *Malita*, or the modern name Malta).[78] Thus, in the Acts Luke is speaking very specifically

[78] This common interpretation of the name *Melítē* is not accepted by Vella. According to him, the island of *Melítē* was inhabited by both Greeks and Phoenicians, and the name is Greek. It

about the island which was well-known to seafarers during Phoenician and later during Punic-Roman times, precisely when Paul's ship was wrecked on the island's coast. The fact that the name seems to have been discovered only upon landing on the island does not necessarily mean that *Melítē* was unheard of by the ship's crew and passengers. As we have seen, it would have been very difficult for them to recognise the island for a number of reasons, including the low-lying coast facing the ENE direction from which they were coming, and the fact that the *Gregale* gales are accompanied by low stratocumulus clouds and continual drizzle, and are common on a small island like Malta. These intensely compact minute raindrops are accompanied by very strong wind, and thus create a kind of misty and cloudy atmosphere which greatly diminishes visibility. The sailors could not possibly recognise the island from the sea, since they had never been to the island before, and there were no particular landmarks on Malta, since the only inhabited town of the island, namely *Melítē*, lay in the interior on the hilly Rabat-Dingli plateau, where Rabat and Mdina stand today. Given this description of the particular nature of the rain and wind during a *Gregale* storm, it was no wonder that the island was unrecognisable. It was not so because it was fairly unknown, as Đurđević wants us to believe regarding Mljet, against the well-known island of *Melítē*, but simply because of adverse weather conditions that rendered visibility very poor and the island's features unrecognisable.

The inhabitants of *Melítē* are described as being βάρβαροι, a word generally taken to refer to natives who could not speak Greek or Latin. In fact, the Maltese natives spoke a Punic dialect as well as Greek. However, the Greek term could also have been derived from Punic *barr*, which would imply simply sons of peasants. This interesting thesis was presented by the Maltese linguist and patriot Mikiel Anton Vassalli (1764-1829),[79] and shows that, although the Maltese natives were simple folk, farmers and peasants, and spoke a Punic dialect, it does not necessarily follow that they were totally ignorant of Greek. Malta and Gozo each were a Roman *municipium*, and it was very natural that Greek would

---

refers to the nymph called *Melitē* and which came to be associated with Malta, formerly called *Thrinacia*, the last place Odysseus landed on before coming to the island of Calypso. There is no source to Phoenician *Maleth*. The Greeks in eastern Sicily were closer to Malta than the Phoenicians in western Sicily. See VELLA (2012), 5.

[79] VELLA (2012), 7: "The Maltese farmers that gave hospitality to St Paul (*Acts* 28.2) were not necessarily ignorant of Greek, as has always been the interpretation of the word *barbaroi* attributed to them, made to mean 'non- Greek speaking', but, as the forgotten Mikiel Anton Vassalli explained better, more than two centuries ago, to mean *'bar barr'*, that is, 'children of the countryside' in Semitic languages. We remind ourselves here of the Biblical *Bar Jonah*, that is, 'son of Jonah', and *Ħamiem il-bar*, that is, 'Pigeons of the countryside', or 'wild pigeons'." One can also add a reference to the Maltese word "barra", which means "outside."

have been known.[80] If their native language has a substratum of Phoenician and Punic, which was later to be amalgamated within the semitic Arabic influence, which is still preponderant in the language, at the same time they had contacts with Greek during Roman and Byzantine times, just as later on they were influenced by other Romance languages like Sicilian, French and Spanish, during the Norman, Angevin, and Aragonese domination, and especially during the times of the Knights of St. John, to be finally colonised by the British, with the influence of English in the language. The geographical position of the islands as a crossroads of cultures between Europe and North Africa has marked the speaking patterns of the Maltese during the course of their long history. So it is no wonder that the barbarian natives of Acts 28:2 could also speak Greek, and that the term βάρβαροι does not imply, as Đurđević insisted, that they were ignorant of classical languages and that therefore the inhabitants of *Melítē* who welcomed Paul and his companions with so much kindness, were not the Maltese, but the natives of *Melita Illyrica*, or Mljet.

The natives showed "unusual kindness" to Paul and his companions. Luke states that "they made us all welcome by lighting a huge fire because it had started to rain and the weather was cold." This reference to the climatic conditions in Malta at the time of the shipwreck is quite interesting. Malta has a typically Mediterranean climate, with long and warm summers, and mild and wet winters. The average temperature in January is 13°C. This can hardly be called "cold". If Paul arrived in Malta in November, the average temperature would have been even higher. However, November is considered to be the wettest month in Malta since the rains tend to fall in late autumn and early spring. The fact that it was raining meant that the relative humidity was quite high, and coupled with the gale force wind, this could produce chilly and damp weather. The survivors had to swim to make it safely to land. So, they were wet with seawater and soaked with the rain. No wonder it felt cold. Indeed, when the *Gregale* wind blows accompanied by incessant rain, it is not at all comfortable to stay outside, and one is literally soaked to the bone and feels cold.

The natives lit a huge fire to warm up the survivors. This would mean that they could make use of abundant quantities of wood. This could raise a problem, since Malta is normally considered to be a barren and treeless island, because it is fairly windswept. However, the island could have had many trees during Roman times and the sheltered valleys and plains in the northern section of the island do provide excellent conditions for all kinds of Mediterranean vegetation, like the Mediterranean pine and the olive tree. Indeed, specialised studies have shown that

---

[80] I thank Profs. Vella for drawing my attention to the fact that the Maltese were Greek-Punic as the Cypriots were Greek-Turkish. The Romans failed to Latinize Malta and Gozo, despite staying here for centuries. For this reason, the transition to the Byzantines came as natural.

the Burmarrad region, which is quite close to Saint Paul's Bay, abounded with olive trees during the Punic-Roman era,[81] so much so that the traditional place of Publius' country villa at *San Pawl Milqi* in Burmarrad is considered by archaeologists to have been an agricultural establishment for the cultivation and pressing of olives. This factor is important to understand that wood must have been plentiful in Malta during Roman times, more so because even the climate itself would have been less arid and maybe less torrid than it is nowadays. The Holocene glacial retreat is dated to around 11,700 years ago. From that point onwards, with the deglaciation of large parts of Europe, the climate gradually developed into its current patterns. Two millennia ago might not look to be a long time for climate change (if we prescind from the current devastating effects of climate change, which are much more recent), but certainly could have played a role in presenting a situation where the Mediterranean winters could have been longer, cooler and damper than they are today, with the effect of a lush vegetation in what nowadays are considered to be arid areas of the Mediterranean (Sicily, Malta, and North Africa).

At this point, we arrive at the most interesting part of the narrative, namely, the mentioning of the viper which attached itself to Paul's hand after it woke up from its lethargy by the heat of the fire that the inhabitants had lit to warm up the survivors.[82] We have, at this point, to make a short reference to the species of serpents present nowadays in Malta, in order to try to understand what kind of serpent, or viper, bit Paul, and why the inhabitants considered it to be lethal and expected Paul to swell up and die instantly.

According to Herpetofauna experts, there are four species of snakes in Malta, only two of which are endemic, whereas another two have become naturalised. The two endemic species are the *Elaphe Situla Leopardina*, or Leopard Snake (in Maltese *Lifgħa*) and the *Coluber Viridiflavus Carbonarius,* or Black Whip Snake (in Maltese *Serp Iswed*). The other two species are believed to have arrived on the island with shipments of fire-wood during the First World War, even though some believe that at least one of them might be originally indigenous. They are the

---

[81] B. Gambin et Alii, (2016) (accessed 5 December 2017). In the abstract the author states: "During the early Roman occupation period, the landscape remains generally open with a moderate increase in *Olea*. This increase corresponds to archaeological evidence for olive oil production in the area, along with increases in cultivated crop *taxa* and associated ruderal species, as well as a rise in fire events. The Maltese archipelago provides important insight into vegetation, human impacts, and climatic changes in an island context during the Holocene."

[82] L.T. Johnson (1992), 462: "The Greek *echidna* refers generally to snakes or vipers. It is used metaphorically for wicked folk in Luke 3:7 (compare Matt 3:7; 12:34; 23:33). The Greek does not describe a 'strike' so much as a 'gripping' (*kathepsen*). It is useless to pursue herptological questions (what sort of snake/viper was it, for example) for which we have no real means of finding answers. The perceptions reported are in any case not of a scientific character."

Telescopus Fallax, or Cat Snake (in Maltese *Serp*), and the *Coluber Florulentus Algirus,* or Algerian Whip Snake (in Maltese *Serp Alġerin*).[83]

The so-called viper which fastened itself to Paul's arm is considered to have been the Leopard Snake, in Maltese called *Lifgħa*, meaning viper. The snake is nocturnal and often hides in shaded valleys and among tree branches. If it were the snake that attached itself to Paul's hand after it was aroused by the heat of the fire that the inhabitants lit, this is another proof that the northwest section of Malta must have been covered with lush vegetation at the time of the arrival of Saint Paul.

It is not easy to explain how the author of Acts could have considered a snake in *Melítē* to be poisonous. However, on a closer analysis of the biblical text, there is nothing to suggest that Luke wants us to conclude that Paul was bitten by a poisonous viper. It was the inhabitants of the island who thought that he would swell up and die, but not as a direct result of the viper itself, but rather because of "divine justice" or δίκη. In Greek mythology *Díkē* was the goddess of justice and moral order. It also meant simply "justice." She was daughter of Zeus and Themis. While *Díkē* represented justice based on socially enforced norms and conventional justice, and was therefore closely linked with human justice, *Themis* was the representation of divine justice. *Díkē* was represented as a young woman holding a balance scale. Her Roman counterpart, *Justitia*, was also represented the same way but was also blindfolded.

The Maltese natives were pagans, and they were fairly familiar with Greek deities. Maybe the mention of *Díkē* on the part of Luke might refer to the Phoenician deity *Sydyk*, righteousness or justice, which would be the equivalent of the Greek *Díkē*. The natives would have mentioned a god or goddess by its name in the Punic dialect, and the author of Acts would have rendered its Greek translation and equivalent. For these simple natives, the power of the gods to reward or punish men for their good deeds or transgressions was a well-established belief. In the case of Paul, the fact that a snake attached itself to his arm suggested to them that he must have been a criminal, since "divine justice" would not let him live, but then they changed their minds and said that he was a god, since he suffered no physical harm. Hence, the insistence of Luke in Acts is not upon the actual fact of the viper

---

[83] MALTA HERPETOLOGICAL SOCIETY http://mhs.org.mt/Knowledgebase/localfauna (accessed 5 December 2017);

http://www.shadowservices.com/nature/Maltese/biology/snakes.htm (accessed 5 December 2017). S. MIFSUD (2014), argues that there are no venomous snakes in Malta that are capable of killing a human being, even though the traditionalists still defend the thesis of the venomous nature of the Elaphe Situla Leopardina (Lifgħa, or Viper in Maltese), that was miraculously rendered innocuous by Paul, when the venom miraculously disappeared from all snakes on the island. For this reason, he prefers the thesis that Mljet (Melita Illyrica) was the island where Paul landed, since it was infested by the dangerous and venomous Vipera ammodytes, until 1910 when Asian mongooses were introduced to control the snake population.

as being poisonous or innocuous, but rather he is giving a theological interpretation of a natural phenomenon, as seen through the eyes of natives who were still living in the superstitious beliefs of paganism, but who thus showed themselves already willing to accept the revelation of the truth that Paul would certainly announce to them during the course of his stay on *Melítē*.

Another plausible explanation can be simply that the venomous viper that bit Saint Paul on *Melítē* is now extinct. Indeed, the Acts use the term ἔχιδνα, which would imply a venomous snake. Smith comes up with the following possibility:

> "The difficulty here is that, although there are serpents in Malta, they are not venomous, as the term ἔχιδνα (viper) implies. Upon this point, I would merely observe that no person, who has studied the changes which the operations of man has produced on the Fauna of any country, will be surprised that a particular species of reptiles should have disappeared from that of Malta ... Perhaps there is nowhere a surface of equal extent in so artificial a state as that of Malta is, at the present day, and nowhere has the aboriginal forest been more completely cleared; but it by no means follows that this was the case when Saint Luke wrote. Indeed we have proof that it was not, for the narrative informs us that the animal came out of a bundle of sticks which Saint Paul had gathered. We need not, therefore, be surprised that with the disappearance of the woods, the noxious reptiles which infested them should also have disappeared."[84]

The judgment of the natives regarding Paul as first being a criminal and then a god is typical of simple folk. The Maltese natives seem to have been influenced by superstitious beliefs in divine vengeance and retribution for evil actions. For whoever knows the history of the Maltese people, such a possibility is not far-fetched. The influence of the priestly caste upon the terrified natives during prehistoric times can be seen in the Neolithic temple culture on the islands, and particularly in the case of the so-called "oracle room" of the Hypogeum at *Ħal Saflieni*. Another interesting fact about the natives' reaction to the viper episode is that Luke's account has other parallels in classical literature.[85] In other words, the aim of the author of Acts is simply that of communicating what the primitive

---

[84] J. Smith (1880), 110-112.

[85] L.T. Johnson (1992), 462: "The translation of *he Díkē* as 'Lady Justice' is necessary because the term here refers not to 'justice' in the philosophical sense, but to 'justice' (*Díkē*) as a personification of retribution or vengeance. A parallel account of a shipwrecked sailor who is saved from the sea only to be killed by a viper is found in the Greek *Anthology* 7:290: 'The shipwrecked mariner had escaped the whirlwind and the fury of the deadly sea, and as he was lying on the Libyan sand, not far from the beach, deep in his last sleep, naked and exhausted by the unhappy wreck, a baleful viper (*echnis*) slew him. Why did he struggle with the waves in vain, escaping then the fate that was his on the land?'" Prof Vella informed me that he knew of a passage in Greek literature describing a dangerous and arduous sea voyage very close to the account in Saint Luke. It is clear that the author of The Acts was knowledgeable of Greek literature enough to adapt extracts to his work. In Classics a branch has arisen investigating the classical style of Biblical Greek literature.

natives of the island thought about the viper episode, without necessarily wanting to enter into the merit of whether the viper was truly poisonous or not, or whether Paul shook it off and miraculously rendered it and all the other vipers on the island innocuous.

"In that neighbourhood there were estates belonging to the chief man of the island, whose name was Publius. He received us and entertained us hospitably for three days." The picture now unfolds in a second moment, when Paul and his 275 companions are welcomed by the τῷ πρώτῳ τῆς νήσου ὀνόματι Ποπλίῳ, the chief man, or president, of the island. We have already considered the meaning of the Greek term *prōtos*, particularly in the analyses by Đurđević and Ciantar. What is of interest to us at this point is the reference to the vicinity of the country estates of Publius to the place of the shipwreck. According to tradition, which dates back some centuries, the estates of Publius were to be found at Burmarrad, close to Salina Bay and to Saint Paul's Bay. Indeed, during Roman times, one could clearly see both bays from the elevated position of what is supposed to be Publius' country estate, namely *San Pawl Milqi* at Burmarrad, just beneath Wardija Ridge. In Roman times, the harbour at Salina Bay would have extended further inland in the direction of the low hill on which the church of *San Pawl Milqi* stands.

The *Missione Archeologica Italiana*, under the direction of Michelangelo Cagiano de Azevedo of the Catholic University of Milan, conducted archaeological studies on the site of *San Pawl Milqi* after 1962. Its findings included the remains of the first church, an *ecclesia Sancti Pauli ta Bindichi*, built on the site in 1448, and subsequently changed to the present church, built in 1647. The place was also known as *Ben Warrat*, hence the modern name Burmarrad. The reference to the meeting of Saint Paul with Publius on this site goes back to 1679, during the pastoral visit of Bishop Molina, but this does not mean that the tradition started then. Another tradition points to the church of *San Ġwann tal-Ħereb*, on the Wardija Ridge further up from Burmarrad, where other Roman remains have been discovered. What is quite interesting is the extent of the country villa, which was an agricultural establishment for the pressing of olives. According to the Maltese art historian Mario Buhagiar, "the villa at *San Pawl Milqi* is the largest and most impressive Roman agricultural plan so far known to the Maltese Islands. Its greatest significance lies in the installations for the extraction and processing of olive oil."[86]

The same art historian mentions another important site, to which we have already referred, namely the *Fanum Iunonis* at *Tas-Silġ*, where there are the remains of a Byzantine Christian basilica and also of an agricultural establishment, upon much older remains going back to the era of the Neolithic temple builders and to

[86] M. Buhagiar (1996), 15-30.

Phoenician and Punic remains. This site is geographically close to the Munxar reef, in the outer reaches of Saint Thomas Bay, on the southeast coast of Malta, which is another possible site for the shipwreck, according to more recent, albeit non-scientific, analyses. Given that the majority of scholars opt for the northern part of Malta as having been the site of the shipwreck, the ubication of *San Pawl Milqi* seems to be more acceptable, at least as an indication that a large Roman agricultural establishment existed in this area, where 276 persons could have been given hospitality by the *prōtos* of the island, had this villa truly belonged to him.

"It happened that Publius' father was in bed, suffering from fever and dysentery. Paul went in to see him, and after a prayer he laid his hands on the man and healed him." The Acts here portray Paul performing one of the important apostolic ministries underlined in Mk 16:16-17: "These are the signs that will be associated with believers: in my name they will cast out devils; they will have the gift of tongues; they will pick up snakes in their hands and be unharmed should they drink deadly poison; they will lay their hands on the sick, who will recover." Indeed, the Acts portray Paul as doing just this in Malta, namely laying his hands upon sick people and healing them. This seems an insignificant detail, when compared to what the apostle did in many of his other missionary journeys. However, its weight in the narrative is very important, when one considers the effects of tradition that has attributed to Paul the evangelisation of the Maltese natives.

For now, we concentrate upon the healing of Publius' father. The "fever and dysentery" from which he was suffering can nowadays be scientifically proved and indicated and provide a very reliable proof regarding Malta as the island where Paul was shipwrecked. One of the most widespread infections in Malta, at least until the mid-20th century, was *Brucellosis*, a highly contagious condition caused by ingestion of unpasteurised milk or undercooked meat from infected animals, primarily goats. Because it was endemic to Malta, where goats abounded, the disease was known as *Brucellosis Melitensis* or "Malta fever." It was David Bruce who first studied the disease in 1887. Later on, in 1905, a Maltese medical doctor and archaeologist, Sir Themistocles Zammit, identified unpasteurised milk as the major source for this disease.[87]

This could explain why "when this happened, the other sick people on the island also came and were cured." The illness was rampant on the island, as well as various other kinds of disease and must have been a major source of concern. In this way, the power of healing of the apostle became evident and news spread like wildfire among the local inhabitants. But what is even more important is the fact that Paul prayed and lay his hands upon Publius' father, and supposedly also on the other natives. One can "compare the account at the beginning of Jesus' ministry,

[87] H.V. Wyatt (2005), 451-454.

when the healing of Peter's mother-in-law of a fever turns into a general press of the populace to be healed of a variety of illnesses (Luke 4:38-44)."[88]

It comes as very natural to ask: if Paul healed so many natives as soon as he set foot on the island, what could he not have done during his three-month stay on the island of *Melítē*? According to local tradition Paul was confined to a grotto in the town of *Melítē*, but we do know that Paul was not treated like a prisoner during his arrest and journey to Rome, and in Malta he earned his own liberty and could roam about freely. After all, where could Paul escape from an island during the winter months when no navigation was available because of the adverse weather? The fact that Paul could have evangelised the natives of Malta is not documented in the Acts narrative, but this does not mean that it did not happen. The Acts can be interpreted as stating that Paul cured the inhabitants of *Melítē*, but not on the same day. Again, Luke did not have an intention to go into details in a moment of transition in Paul's life journey. He was keen in presenting Paul giving witness to Christ in Rome. Yet, he does give us a clue at the end of the narrative. "They honoured us with many marks of respect, and when we sailed, they put on board the provisions we needed."

What does this gesture of respect and generosity imply? The islanders had to provide for the sustenance of the crew and prisoners who were 276 persons in all for three whole months, and then they loaded the ship with provisions when these departed at the reopening of the season of navigation, probably around March 61 A.D.[89]

This last detail is very important in our conjectural analysis of the narrative. The generosity of the natives must surely have been the result of a service of kindness and human concern on the part of the 276 guests towards the local population. Now we know, from the narrative of the gale, that Paul assumed an important role among crew and passengers during the crucial moments of the epic journey. No wonder that, with the divine power of healing exercised in favour of the locals on the island of *Melítē*, Paul must have been able to preach the Gospel, as he would certainly have done in all the places he visited. He had ample time to do so, three whole months.

---

[88] L.T. Johnson (1992), 463.

[89] L.T. Johnson (1992), 463: "*They paid us many honours*. The translation of *pollaîs timaîs etímēsan* is uncertain, since it can refer either to honour or to payment/price. Luke tends to use the term in the monetary sense. Despite that, the translation chooses 'honours' since the next phrase spells out the gift of possessions. *They gave us the things we needed*. The general meaning is clear, but the precise translation is uncertain: *epitithēmi* could be taken in the physical sense: 'as we were sailing away (*anagoménois*), they put on board the things we needed (*tà pròs tàs chreías*),' or could be taken in the broader sense, they 'bestowed.' As always in Luke-Acts, the sharing of physical possessions is a symbol of sharing in the good news (Luke 6:32-36; 8:3; 12:32-34; 14:13-14; 18:22; 21:1-4; Acts 2:42-47; 4:32-37)."

The local traditions linked with the presence of the Apostle Paul on Malta, which are thought to be late pious inventions made up by the Order of St. John in order to enhance the cult of Saint Paul for the benefit and glory of the same Order which governed Malta, might not be so biased as they are normally presented. Traditions are not born out of nothing. Although the Acts narrative is very succinct in its presentation of what Paul actually did on *Melítē*, it gives us enough elements to arrive at the origins of a Christian faith in Malta dating from Apostolic times. This certainly does not imply the establishment of an organised ecclesiastical framework on the model of Ciantar's description, with Publius as having been ordained bishop by Saint Paul, or the transformation of Publius' palace in *Melítē* (Mdina) as the cathedral church of the island. What it does imply, however, is that Christ was proclaimed in Malta by Paul himself, and the natives reacted positively to this good news by showing a sincere witness of Christian charity that was already rooted in their pagan culture and took a new form when Paul departed from them.

We shall now proceed to take a brief look at the traditional places associated with the presence of Saint Paul on the island of Malta. We have already referred to some of them. Our aim is not that of proving their historical link with the physical presence of Saint Paul, but rather of proving that the devotional value of these places is a proof of a long Christian tradition present on the island of Malta, tracing its origins to the day when the barbarian natives welcomed 276 survivors from a shipwreck on the coast of their island home.

Places associated with the cult of Saint Paul in Malta

The presence of Christian archaeological remains on the island of Malta does not go back to the 1st century AD.[90] The earliest vestiges of Christian places of cult are the catacombs, concentrated largely in Rabat, but also present in other areas of the island, and the troglodyte churches during Roman-Byzantine times, that is around the 4th century. The most famous example of such troglodyte chapels is the cave of the *Madonna tal-Mellieħa*, although the fresco of the Virgin and Child is dated to not earlier than the 14th century. Indeed, the Mellieħa Ridge has yielded some fine examples of early Byzantine-Siculo troglodyte settlements, in which one always finds a place dedicated to cult, and hence a rock-cut church. The troglodyte settlement of San Niklaw[91] is one such example. Other examples in Malta include the San Leonardo cave-church above Wied Liemu, Limits of Rabat,

---

[90] M. Buhagiar (1983), 291-298; A. Messina (1989) 109-120; M. Buhagiar (1998) 221-238; M. Buhagiar, (2002) 253-283.

[91] K. Buhagiar (1997), 131-138.

and the Mensija cave-church in modern-day San Ġwann, also dedicated to Saint Leonard of Limoges.

It is within these categories of cultic places, namely catacombs and cave-churches, that the principal sanctuaries linked with the presence of Saint Paul in Malta are to be found. At this stage, we shall not repeat what we have already stated regarding many of the places mentioned as being linked with the presence of Saint Paul, but it is important to make a list of them in order to have a general view of the widespread devotion to the Apostle that has been present in Malta at least since mediaeval times,[92] and most probably with origins in the Roman-Byzantine era before the Arab domination of the islands.

The places traditionally linked with the presence of Saint Paul in Malta include, first and foremost, the Grotto of Saint Paul, which is a rock-cut church within the complex of catacombs outside the walls of the ancient town of *Melítē*, in modern-day Rabat. To this prime sanctuary of cult and devotion towards Saint Paul we shall give particular importance.

The next place which has been linked to the Apostle's arrival at least since mediaeval times is the area of Saint Paul's Bay and Salina Bay, together with Burmarrad and the Wardija Ridge, where we find the greatest concentration of places of cult associated with Saint Paul. Foremost among them is the church of *San Pawl tal-Ħġejjeġ*, marking the most ancient among the traditional places deemed to have been the spot where the Maltese natives welcomed Paul after his shipwreck. Further inland, the church of *San Pawl Milqi*, with the Roman remains of the agricultural establishment reputed to have been Publius' country villa, is another important place of cult associated with Saint Paul since mediaeval times. Other places of minor importance can be found in the same area, like the Apostle's spring, or *Għajn ir-Rażul*, on the opposite side of Xemxija, and the church of *San Ġwann tal-Ħereb*, above the Wardija Ridge, where a Roman stone trough is reputed to have been used as a baptismal font by the Apostle (the "font" used to stand beside the church of *San Xmun ta' Wied Qannotta*, close by).

There are at least two other churches dedicated to Saint Paul, above the Great Fault, or Victoria Lines. These churches are traditionally considered as places where the Apostle stopped and from where he preached. One is the church of *San Pawl tat-Tarġa* in Naxxar. The other church is that of *San Pawl tal-Qlejgħa*, close to Mosta, which simply marks the way that led from Burmarrad to the town of *Melítē*, following the *wadi* that from the Rabat plateau descends to Salina Bay.

A more recent natural sanctuary dedicated to the Apostle Paul is, of course, the islet of *Selmunett*, with the statue of the Apostle, which marks the place where popular tradition holds that the Apostle was shipwrecked. The tradition is

---

92 S. Fiorini - H.C.R. Vella (2006), 161-172; S. Fiorini (2010), 83-97.

fairly recent and does not go beyond the 19th century, but since the islet has been considered to be the traditional place of the shipwreck, it can be included within the list of cultic places linked with Saint Paul. Indeed, as we have seen, Smith places the scene of the shipwreck quite close to this islet, by stating that "the place where two seas meet" is precisely the narrow and shallow channel separating the islet from the mainland.

Although we shall not describe any other places related to Saint Paul's presence, it is important to refer to the three main churches on the island that are dedicated to Saint Paul and to particular events of his life. I refer to the Cathedral Church of Mdina, reputed to have been built upon the very place where Publius had his palace. Since Norman times, it was dedicated to Saint Paul, and its titular painting depicts the Conversion of the Apostle by Mattia Preti (1613-1699). The mediaeval cathedral had a beautiful Polyptych as its main altarpiece, depicting Saint Paul with scenes of his life. The Polyptych is attributed to the circle of the Catalan Luis Borassa (1360-1426) and is fortunately preserved in good condition in the Cathedral Museum. The Collegiate Church of Saint Paul in Rabat, built adjacent to Saint Paul's Grotto in 1653-1683 over the remains of another church built in 1578 upon the mediaeval *ecclesia Sancti Pauli de crypta*, is dedicated to the Martyrdom of the Apostle, but its titular painting, by Stefano Erardi (1678), depicts the shipwreck scene. The Collegiate Church of the Shipwreck of Saint Paul in Valletta was built in 1582 in the new city of the Knights without any historical link to a place sanctified by the presence of the Apostle. Its titular painting, depicting the scene of the shipwreck, is the work of Matteo Perez d'Aleccio (1547-1616).

The Grotto of Saint Paul in Rabat

The venerated Grotto of Saint Paul in Rabat is the most important devotional place in Malta associated with the presence of the Apostle Paul.[93] According to a purely devotional tradition, Paul resided in this man-made cave during the course of his three-month stay on the island.[94] The cave or crypt is situated close to the old city walls of *Melítē*, and the whole complex of later buildings, including the parish church of Rabat, the church of Saint Publius and the underlying Grotto of St. Paul were originally known, at least in 1436, as *Cappella di San Paulu di Fora,* that is, outside the walls of *Melítē*, or what later became known as Mdina.

The Grotto was already venerated during mediaeval times. Its importance in antiquity is disputed, although it lies close to the Catacombs of Saint Paul, in an

---

93 M. Buhagiar (1990), 51-64; W.L. Zammit (2006), 219-235.

94 J. Cassar Pullicino (1944), 19-31.

area which is important from the point of view of Paleo-Christian underground remains.

The Grotto is mentioned as a place of devotion in the Report of the Apostolic Visitation of Mgr Pietro Dusina (1575):

> "On the same day after lunch he visited the parish church outside the walls which is located in Rabat and which is known as Saint Paul's church [...] This same place in which the Church has been founded is a holy place, and it is very devout since Saint Paul dwelt in it, and often preached here the Word of God. The church is entirely dug in the living rock. The faithful daily take fragments from the rock, since they say that this rock is powerful against all kinds of poison if one mixes the fragments with water and drinks them. This grace is given in honour of Saint Paul who lived in that great rock cave, so much is God wonderful in his Saints."[95]

This is one of the many witnesses to the devotional value of the Grotto of Saint Paul,[96] and to the tradition of the *Terra sigillata Melitensis*, which used to be exported all over Europe as a remedy for snake bites and other kinds of illness associated with poison.[97] We have already seen how Đurđević dismisses such a tradition as a fake and a pure invention on the part of the Maltese to enhance devotion to Saint Paul's presence on *Melita Africana*.

The cave church was visited by pilgrims, but devotion sometimes waned. It was only in 1615 that we witness the beginning of a new era for the crypt of Saint Paul. From Bishop Baldassare Cagliares, who was on pastoral visitation, we know that a Spanish hermit had been living in the cave church. His name was Juan Benegas de Cordoba,[98] who had been living there since 1600. In 1610 he received the Grotto under his care from the Rabat parish, and then ceded the holy place to Grand Master Alof Wignacourt in 1617. Wignacourt built the Church of Saint Publius above the venerated Grotto. The church was rebuilt in 1692 and 1726. Thus, it became part of

---

[95] G. Aquilina – S. Fiorini (ed). (2001), [f. 26v-27] 51: "Eodem die post prandium visitavit ecclesiam parrochialem extra moenia sub vocabulo Sancti Pauli sitam in Rabato [...] Locus iste in quo Ecclesia fundata est, sanctus est, et valde devotus quia in eo divus Paulus habitavit, et sæpe Verbum Dei prædicavit, ecclesia est tota in saxo posita, ex qua fideles quotidie fragmenta eripiunt quæ dicunt adversus omnia venena prodesse, si aqua immista bibantur hanc gratiam in honorem divi Pauli fuisse concessam illi saxo permagno in quo ipse habitavit, ità mirabilis est Deus in Sanctis suis."

[96] Quintinus describes the ancient cult of Saint Paul at the Grotto: Vella (1980), 45-47: "Near the city there is a cave dug in a rock, with two altars within; they say that Paul was in custody in it for three months along with the other prisoners, healing at the same time the islanders who were vexed with various kinds of sickness and diseases, and calling them to Christ by his preaching [...] From that cave, which I have just mentioned, pieces of stones are daily cut off by visitors who confirm openly throughout Africa, Italy and Rome that they are healed from the bites of serpents and scorpions through these stones. The people consider this as a favour from Saint Paul."

[97] Th. Freller (2006), 191-218.

[98] J. Azzopardi (2006), 173-190.

the whole complex of the new Church of Saint Paul, finished in 1683 by Lorenzo Gafà, and built through the munificence of the Noble Lady Guzmana Navarra, on the plans of architect Francesco Buonamici.[99]

The Church of *San Pawl tal-Ħġejjeġ* in Saint Paul's Bay

This church is indicated as the most likely place commemorating the shipwreck of Saint Paul and his arrival in Malta. It stands on the eastern coast of Saint Paul's Bay, some distance from Wignacourt Tower. Unfortunately, the ancient church was bombed during the war and a new church now stands on the same spot, built according to the same dimensions and layout of the old church, with the typical portico surrounding it, meant to provide shelter for pilgrims on visit to the sanctuary.

The origins of the church are ancient, but no written records exist. What is certain is that the church gave the name to the bay, namely *Cala di San Paolo*, and marked the long tradition that the Apostle had been shipwrecked on those shores. According to the acts of Notary Luca Sillato, the church was rebuilt in 1441 and was endowed with a pious benefice by the Dean of the Cathedral Chapter of Mdina. The notarial deed states, *quivi è una Chiesa di molta veneratione*.[100] The same church is mentioned by Quintinus in 1536, who identifies the *locus bimaris*, "the place between two seas", by the church.[101] The church stands on a slight elevation overlooking a shallow promontory (where the Gillieru restaurant stands) This jut of land would mark the *dithálassos*, and separated the beach on both sides. The western side of the beach is now occupied by a small harbour (*Il-Menqa*).

Pietro Dusina mentions this church and the *Cala di San Paolo* in his Apostolic Visitation. When describing the rural churches of the village of *Mellieħa*, he mentions the "church of Saint Paul by the sea, marking the place where Saint Paul arrived after his shipwreck. This church was built in his honour and has given the name to the place which is known as the *Cala di San Paolo*."[102]

It was Grand Master Alof de Wignacourt (10 February 1601 – 14 September 1622) who undertook the rebuilding of this church and the tower further away from

---

99 *St. Publius Sanctuary. The Wignacourt*: http://thewignacourt.com/posts/st-publiuss-sanctuary/index.html (accessed 11 December 2017).

100 J. Galea (1990), 69-74.

101 The Latin text of Quintinus is found in Vella (1980), 44: "Hoc sibi modo Paulum astruunt nautae Melitenses; cuius insuper vestigis non in uno loco demonstrant et adorant. Visitur litus loci illius bimaris [...]; nunc a Paulo hic vetustissimae cognominatum, in quod is navem illisit. Ibi non ultimae venerationis aedicula lapide extructa."

102 G. Aquilina – S. Fiorini (ed). (2001), [f. 181^{v}] 187: "Ecclesia Sancti Pauli prope litus maris, quo divus Paulus post eius naufragium primo pervenit, ad cuius honorem fuit erecta dicta Ecclesia, et datum nomen dicti loci quod vocatur la Cala di San Paolo."

it, in honour of Saint Paul, to whom he held particular devotion, being a member of the Langue of France, whose patron saint was Saint Paul. After having received the approval of the Grand Council of the Order in 1609, Wignacourt proceeded to build a watch tower in the *Cala di San Paolo*. The new Chapel of Saint Paul was rebuilt some distance away in the place where it now stands. The plans for the tower and maybe also for the church were made by Vittorio Cassar, son of the well-known Maltese architect and engineer Girolamo Cassar. The foundation stone of the church was laid in 1610 with the participation of the Grand Master and Bishop. The church was finished in 1617, when Grand Master Wignacourt, in a deed drawn by Notary Giovanni Tholossenti, created a College of Canons to officiate the Grotto of Saint Paul in Rabat and this new church, which he joined to the same College, after the concession that the Spanish hermit Juan Benegas, who lived as a hermit in the Grotto of Saint Paul, had made to the Order. The College of Canons was obliged to celebrate the feast of Saint Paul annually in the church of Saint Paul on Sexagesima Sunday, which falls roughly in February. Maybe this is the reason why the feast of the Shipwreck of Saint Paul began to be celebrated on 10 February, the day on which Grand Master Wignacourt was elected and a date which is also close to Sexagesima Sunday. In fact, the date rather marks a period close to the departure of Saint Paul from Malta, since the shipping lanes were closed roughly between November and February, and Paul had wintered on the island. The *Cala di San Paolo* is considered as the place of the shipwreck, but it does not follow that Paul departed from Malta from this place.[103]

The Church of *San Pawl Milqi*

We have already mentioned this church in other parts of our presentation, as marking the place where, according to popular tradition, Paul and his other 275 companions were welcomed and given hospitality for three days by the chief man of the island, Publius, and where Paul cured Publius' father from fever and dysentery. The church stands upon the remains of a Roman country villa, which was excavated in 1963-1968 by the *Missione Archeologica Italiana*, and which appears to have been mainly, but not exclusively, used as an agricultural establishment for the pressing of olives, upon a prominent site above the Burmarrad plain and Salina Bay, with signs of human occupation from the 2nd century B.C. to the 4th century A.D.[104]

---

[103] For this reason, if we are to retain 10 February as the Feast of Saint Paul's Shipwreck on Malta, we could state that the date is just a pious tradition, but does not actually indicate the exact time when the Apostle reached our shores, but is rather close to the date when he departed.

[104] A. Bonanno (2005), 298-299.

The church itself is recorded in 1448 as an *ecclesia Sancti Pauli ta Bindichi*. It was rebuilt after 1647, but it was not associated with the cult of Saint Paul in the pastoral visitations of the bishops of Malta. "The first known reference to the story of the meeting on the site between Paul and Publius is in the report of the pastoral visitation to the church of Bishop Gerolamo Molina on 28 May 1679."[105]

The church of *San Pawl Milqi* has a shaft through which one can go down and see some of the remains of the olive presses of the agricultural establishment. Although there is no documentary proof that this was Publius' villa or that Saint Paul ever set foot in this place, popular tradition and veneration developed over the centuries based on the fact that the villa stands on elevated ground from where, before the modern development of the high-rise apartments of Qawra and Buġibba, which today obstruct the view, one could easily see Salina Bay, Qawra Point, and Saint Paul's Bay, and even the islet of Selmunett. If Paul was shipwrecked in this area, the event could easily have been seen by the inhabitants of this villa and environs, supposing that they would have been among the first to offer assistance to Paul and his companions.

Other churches associated with the presence of Saint Paul

The Wardija Ridge is located just above Burmarrad and extends to the inner reaches of Saint Paul's Bay. It seems to have been inhabited during the 1st century A.D., since some remains of Roman agricultural establishments have been found. Among the various churches on these hills from where one gets a splendid view of Saint Paul's Island, we mention just two, which are in a very indirect way linked to the cult of Saint Paul in Malta. The whole area of Wardija was preferred by the Knights of St. John as a country residence, and they built various country mansions and churches that are still in existence.

The church of *San Ġwann tal-Ħereb* was built upon the remains of a Roman agricultural establishment. This church is reputed to be ancient, and that it was built upon the spot where Saint Paul baptised many inhabitants. The tradition of Paul baptising the Maltese is shared between this place and the church of *San Pawl Milqi*, further down. As a sign of the baptismal value of this site, there used to be a large round Roman stone trough close to the church, which was carried some distance away and placed alongside the façade of the church of *San Xmun ta' Wied Qannotta*. According to Bishop Molina, who made a pastoral visitation to the church in 1680, it depended upon the parish of Naxxar. It had been desecrated, but was rebuilt in 1610 by Girolamo Scerri from Naxxar, as Bishop Cagliares testifies

105 M. Buhagiar (1996), 16.

in his pastoral visitation in 1617. The present church was built by Count Niccolò Sciberras Bologna in 1852.[106]

The church of *San Pawl tat-Tarġa* is dedicated to Saint Paul and is situated on the Great Fault (hence the Maltese name *Tarġa*, meaning "step") in Naxxar, overlooking Salina Bay. According to another popular but unproven tradition, the name Naxxar derives from *Nassara*, which means Christians (*Insara* in Maltese), for the simple reason that the inhabitants of the village were the first Maltese who welcomed Paul's preaching.

The Apostolic Visitator Pietro Dusina mentions an *ecclesiam sub vocabilis Sancti Pauli constructam in medio casalis Nasciari*,[107] which cannot be the same one, since the church of *San Pawl tat-Tarġa* does not stand in the centre of the town of Naxxar, but on the edge of the Great Fault. The church is certainly an ancient one, but in 1618 it was desecrated by Bishop Baldassare Cagliares. In 1699 a new church was built during the time of Bishop Davide Cocco Palmieri. The stone statue of Saint Paul in front of the chapel was made in 1770.

The devotional place of the Shipwreck on Selmunett

We have already described in detail the theory of Paul's shipwreck in the whereabouts of the islet of Selmunett. As we have already stated, the tradition linking the shipwreck to this place is not an ancient one. It was in 1844 that a stone statue of the Apostle Paul was placed on the islet, the work of Sigismondo and Salvatore Dimech. The statue was blessed in 1845 and has been restored more than once, since it lies on top of a windswept rock and suffers from the ravages of winter-gales and sea spray. The islet, however, already had a watch tower built around 1649 by Grand Master Jean Paul Lascaris Castellar, and is nowadays sadly in ruins.[108]

Concluding remarks

The aim of this chapter is simply that of mentioning the importance of the cult of Saint Paul in Malta, with the help of various places associated with the presence of the Apostle on the island during his three-month stay. Indeed, judging from the Acts of the Apostles' account, we cannot arrive at any scientific conclusion regarding where exactly Paul was staying on the island, and what he did during that

---

106 A. Ferres (1866), 346-347.

107 G. Aquilina – S. Fiorini (ed). (2001), [f. 38^{v}] 64.

108 *St. Paul's Island*, in https://en.wikipedia.org/wiki/St_Paul%27s_Island (accessed 11 December 2017). S. Farrugia Randon (1995).

lapse of time, except for the initial days of his presence in the house of Publius and his miracles of healing the indigenous inhabitants of the island.

The cult of Saint Paul in Malta is documented since mediaeval times.[109] However, since there are vestiges of Christian places of cult in the troglodyte churches dating also from Byzantine times, as well as the rock-cut catacombs of the town of *Melítē*, dating from the 4th century AD, we can imagine that the tradition linking Malta to Saint Paul goes back further in history, and that the Apostle was surely engaged in evangelising the local population during his stay on the island.[110]

One thing is certain. No other place that is indicated as the island of the shipwreck can boast of so many Pauline memories as the island of Malta. This, coupled with the role of the Order of the Knights of Saint John in enhancing Christian traditions during the period it governed the island, is an indication that needs to be reckoned with when trying to understand the significance of the cult of Saint Paul in Malta.

---

109 An interesting contribution to the study of the cult of Saint Paul in Malta is the publication of the long Greek poem written by an Italo-Byzantine exile in *Melitogaudos* (one of the Byzantine names of Malta and Gozo, the other one being *GaudoMelítē*), transcribed and translated by S. Fiorini and H.C.R. Vella (2006)161-172, particularly the part dedicated to the shipwreck narrative of the Apostle Paul [f. 84v – f. 85] in pages 168-169. The full critical edition of the Italo-Byzantine poem is published in J. Busuttil – S. Fiorini – H.C.R. Vella (2010), [f. 84v – f. 85] 166-169.

110 M. Buhagiar (2006), 155-160.

Conclusion

Is *Melita Illyrica* or *Melita Africana* the place where Saint Paul was shipwrecked on his way to Rome in A.D. 60? The answer to this question has been the aim of this study. Malta and Mljet are both linked to the tradition of the arrival of Saint Paul on their shores. That is why I have chosen the title *Melita Illyrica* and *Melita Africana. The Islands of Saint Paul.*

Being a native of Malta, it is obvious that I would opt for the more convincing proof for my island home as the place where Paul was shipwrecked and spent three months in the winter of A.D. 60-61. After all, indications in Luke's narrative plus the opinion of the majority of biblical scholars and historians have always indicated the island of Malta as the place where Paul providentially stopped on his way to Rome, after he was shipwrecked during an eventful storm. At the same time, I was curiously interested in discovering the other island that boasts of being the place where Paul was shipwrecked, namely, the island of Mljet in the Adriatic, off the coast of Dalmatia, in modern day Croatia.

What could be of interest in this presentation concerns my personal reflection on what I have read and experienced, both in being a native of Malta as well as by visiting the island of Mljet and seeing for myself the memories linked with the supposed visit of the Apostle on that island. My conclusions are the result of my own reflection, and maybe also imagination, on the scant documentary and archaeological evidence present on Malta, and much less on Mljet.

In my analysis I still have to refer to an ancient witness to the event of the shipwreck narrative in Acts 27-28, namely, the commentary of Saint John Chrysostom on the Book of the Acts of the Apostles. I will present here what this eminent Doctor of the Church has to say regarding the island of *Melítē* and its natives who welcomed Paul and his companions:

> "*Showed*, he says, *no little kindness to us—barbarians* (as they were)—*having kindled a fire*: else it were of no use that their lives be saved, if the wintry weather must destroy them. Then Paul having taken brushwood, laid it on the fire. See how active he is; observe how we nowhere find him doing miracles for the sake of doing them, but only upon emergency. Both during the storm when there was a cause he prophesied, not for the sake of prophesying, and here again in the first instance he lays on brushwood:—nothing for vain display, but (with a simple view) to their being preserved, and enjoying some warmth. Then a *viper fastened*

on his hand. And when the barbarians saw the venomous beast hang on his hand, they said among themselves, No doubt this man is a murderer, whom, though he hath escaped the sea, yet vengeance suffereth not to live. (v. 4.) Well also was this permitted, that they should both see the thing and utter the thought, in order that, when the result ensued, there might be no disbelieving the miracle. Observe their good feeling (towards the distressed), in saying this (not aloud, but) among themselves—observe (also) the natural judgment clearly expressed even among barbarians, and how they do not condemn without assigning a reason. And these also behold, that they may wonder the more. *And he shook off the beast into the fire and felt no harm. Howbeit they looked when he should have swollen or fallen down dead suddenly: but after they had looked a great while, and saw no harm come to him, they changed their minds, and said that he was a god.* (v. 5, 6.) They expected him, it says, to fall down dead: and again, having seen that nothing of the kind happened to him, they said, He is a god. Again, another excess on the part of these men. *In the same quarters were possessions of the chief man of the island, whose name was Publius; who received us, and lodged us three days courteously. And it came to pass, that the father of Publius lay sick of a fever and of a bloody flux: to whom Paul entered in, and prayed, and laid his hands on him, and healed him.* (v. 7, 8.) Behold again another hospitable man, Publius, who was both rich and of great possessions: he had seen nothing, but purely out of compassion for their misfortune, he received them, and took care of them. So that he was worthy to receive kindness: wherefore Paul as a requital for his receiving them, *healed him. So when this was done, others also, who had diseases in the island, came, and were healed: who also honoured us with many honours; and when we departed, they laded us with such things as were necessary* (v. 9, 10), both us and the rest. See how when they were quit of the storm, they did not become more negligent, but what a liberal entertainment was given to them for Paul's sake: and three months were they there, all of them provided with sustenance. See how all this is done for the sake of Paul, to the end that the prisoners should believe, and the soldiers, and the centurion. For if they were very stone, yet from the counsel they heard him giving, and from the prediction they had heard him making, and from the miracles they knew him to have wrought, and from the sustenance they by his means enjoyed, they must have got a very high notion of him."[111]

---

[111] Ph. Schaff (2002), 440. Latin translation of the original Greek text of S. Ioannis Chrysostomi, *In Acta Apostolorium,* Hom. LIV, in J.P. Migne, *Patrologia Cursus Completus. Series Graeca*, Vol. 60, col. 373-374: "Cap. 28. v. 1. *Barbari vero præstabant non modicam humanitatem nobis.* 2. *Accensa enim pyra, reficiebant nos omnes, propter imbrem qui imminebat, et frigus.* 3. *Cum congregasset autem Paulus sarmentorum multitudinem et imposiuisset in ignem, vipera a calore cum processisset, momordit manum ejus.* 1. Quomodo humanitatem præstarent barbari, interpretatur: *Accensa,* inquit, *pyra reficiebant nos [omnes].* Quia enim nulla ex evasione utilitas fuisset, cum frigus illos interempturum esset, accendunt pyram. Hinc Paulus accepta sarmenta in rogum infert, ut ille subjungit: *Cum congregasset autem Paulus sarmentorum multitudinem.* Vide illum operantem; et nusquam frustra mirabilia patrantem, sed ob necessitatem: nam in tempestate quoque non sine causa prophetavit, et hic rursum sarmenta colligit et imponit. Vide illum non ad fastum vel superflue agentem, sed ut illi servarentur calore quodam fruentes. Deinde vipera ex calore egressa manum ejus invasit: et quod invaserit, palam est ex sequentibus. 4. *Ut vero viderunt barbari pendentem bestiam de manu ejus, inter se dicebant: Utique homicida est homo hic quem servatum de mari ultio non sinis vivere.* Bene hoc permissum est, ut talia illi viderent et loquerentur, ut futuro miraculo fidem non negarent. Vide naturale judicium a barbaris prolatum, ipsosque honeste inter se loquentes, nec simpliciter damnantes. Ita hic prius vident, ut magis mirentur. 5. 'At ille escussa bestia in ignem, nihil mali passus est: 6.

What Saint John Chrysostom is stating in this commentary is simply that which Luke himself had stated in Acts 28:1-10. Yet there is more to discover if one reflects upon these words. First of all, Chrysostom lays great importance to the attitude of the islanders when they came to know Paul. They were marvelling at his sense of initiative in lending an active hand to add brushwood to the fire, even though he had just escaped a fearful experience of a shipwreck. In the narrative, Paul remains the protagonist, but he is presented through the eyes of the natives. These simple people were terrified of what they were beholding when the viper fastened itself to Paul's hands, when the Apostle just shook it into the fire and suffered no harm. The excess to which they judged Paul went from thinking that he was a criminal to considering the possibility that he was a god. Such an attitude is typical of primitive peoples and cultures, as well as of simple country folk who naïvely believe in fables and legends without any regard for scientific analysis.

The inhabitants of *Melítē* showed these characteristic traits. Yet they were not uncivilised. They would not condemn a man without assigning a reason for his behaviour. This natural way of judging was also linked to their sense of generosity and kind-heartedness in providing for the needs of 276 persons not only during the three days these spent as guests of Publius, but indeed during three whole months, and then lavishly loading the ship with everything these persons needed for their last leg of the journey to Italy.

One wonders how such a way of behaviour could be labelled "barbarian" in the modern sense of the term, when in truth it was a humanitarian gesture of goodwill that was a sign of a willingness to welcome and to share all they possessed. Is not such an attitude a prerequisite for welcoming the gift of the good news of Jesus Christ? Luke does not seem to want to dwell in great length and detail on what truly happened on *Melítē* during those three months. The effect of this silence has been the birth of a strong and seemingly imaginative tradition that has made of Malta a centre of devotion to Saint Paul and a bulwark of Catholicism. We do

---

illi vero existimabant eum in tumorem convertendum et subito casurum mortuum, Diu autem illis expectantibus, et videntibus nihil illi mali accidere, mutata sententia, dicebant ipsum esse deum.' Qui existimabant illum *In tumorum convertendum*, id est, dirumpendum: videntes hi eum nihil mali passum, dicunt esse deum. Rursus supra modum illum honorant, ut turbæ illæ in Lycaonia. 7. *In locis autem vicinis erant prædia principis insulæ nomine Publii; qui nos suscipiens, triduo nos benigne hospitio recepit*. Ecce iterum alius hospitalis Publius dives et opulentus: qui cum nihil vidisset, se ob solam calamitatem misertus illorum, hospitio excepit et fovit. 8. *Contigit autem, patrem Publii febribus ac dysenteria vexatum decumbere: ad quem Paulus ingressus oravit, impositisque illi manibus curavit eum*. Quia dignus erat beneficio, vicem illi hospitalitatis rependens, curavit patrem. 9. *Quo facto, omnes qui in insula habebant infirmitates, accedebant et curabantur:* 10. *qui etiam multis honoribus nos honoraverunt, et solventibus imposuerunt quæ necessaria erant*: id est, et nobis solventibus necessaria dederunt et aliis. Vide illos a tempestate liberatos, non fuisse neglectos; sed etiam propter Paulum liberali hospitio susceptos: per tres enim menses alimenta omnibus suppeditata sunt."

know that such a fact cannot be ascribed to the coming of Saint Paul but it is of a later development. A cursory look at the history of Malta would show its strategic position not only regarding geography and political events in the Mediterranean, but also regarding the defence of the Catholic faith in a period marked by internal and external tensions. Internal tensions regarded the counter-Reformation efforts of the 16th century, with the consequent Baroque glorification of the Catholic faith in art, architecture, music, etc. External tensions had to do with a continued insistence upon the dangers of Islam and the menacing presence of the "infidel" Turks and Barbary corsairs lurking in the Mediterranean. Such a danger never waned in the minds of the Maltese natives, since it was the explicit intention of the ruling class, namely the Knights of Saint John, to keep them aware of this danger to their faith even when the military power of the Turkish armadas had long-since decreased and nearly disappeared during the second half of the 18th century. To create such an ideal condition for the safeguarding of the Catholic interests in the Mediterranean basin needed a genial ability to create a mythological point of reference which would make the Maltese staunch Catholics. Such a reference was found in the shipwreck account of the Apostle Paul on Malta.

Even before this happened, however, we are aware of an ancient Christian tradition in Malta. The clues we possess are scanty and many lacunae in our knowledge still linger on. However, we possess enough evidence to go back at least to Byzantine times. The same is evident on Mljet, but on a lesser scale. What happened before remains a mystery that is only open to speculation. This is what I have done in many parts of my study. I am aware that speculation without documentary proof is not a guarantee for scientific truth. Nevertheless, Malta still has certain elements that have made me wonder whether things have really changed so radically in these two millennia of history.

One thing that has certainly not changed much is the climate pattern of the island. Whoever is familiar with the late autumn storms that sometimes batter the island cannot feel a stranger when reading Luke's narrative. Observing the meteorological phenomena of the *Gregale* wind corresponds very closely to what Luke narrates. Another interesting feature of the narrative, according to my way of seeing things from a purely popular and not scientific level, is the description of the attitude of the natives of *Melítē*. In their simplicity, they judged Paul by extremes. He was either a criminal or a god. One cannot help noticing the typical southern Mediterranean attitude that is not very accustomed to shades of grey in its insistence that every reality is either white or black. I often pinpoint to this fact with a kind of benevolent belief that it is a faithful picture of the "Maltese" character and can indeed be taken as a proof that the natives described by Luke were the barbarians of *Melita Africana*.

The whole question of the location of the shipwreck narrative would have remained fairly in the background had it not been for the controversy ignited during the 18th century by the Croatian Benedictine Abbot Ignjat Đurđević. Although his thesis seems far-fetched and highly imaginative, one cannot help to admire the efforts of this erudite monk in trying to enhance at all costs the prestige of the Republic of Ragusa (Dubrovnik), and that of his own Benedictine Congregation of *Meleda*, particularly of his monastery of Saint Mary on the island of Mljet. Đurđević was aware that his thesis would meet the staunch resistance of the *Philomaltenses*, subjects of the Kingdom of The Two Sicilies through the powerful influence of the Order of the Knights of Saint John. It was an undisputed fact that the Maltese thesis was highly inflated by the turn of events in the beginning of the 17th century, when Grand Master Alof de Wignacourt proceeded to make of Malta an international centre of pilgrimage for the cult of Saint Paul, particularly in the two key places which were supposed to have been sanctified by the presence of the Apostle, namely the *Crypta Sancti Pauli* in Rabat and the *Ecclesia Sancti Pauli* at the *Cala di San Paolo*, marking the place of the shipwreck and first welcome of the Apostle by the Maltese natives.

The polemical nature of Đurđević's treatise prompted Maltese apologists to respond with equal vigour. They had the backing of the Knights of Saint John, a powerful Catholic institution which had received the islands of Malta and Gozo as a fief from Emperor Charles V in 1530. During the 18th century, the Knights had become well established in Malta, to the point of considering themselves as princes in their own domain, even though the archipelago formally formed part of the Kingdom of The Two Sicilies. In order to enhance their prestige as a Catholic institution worthy of note on the political level, the Knights had ensured that the local population would truly become fervently Catholic. They had built cathedrals, churches and private chapels, and commissioned famous artists to embellish these religious monuments. Above all, they had given importance to the figure of Saint Paul as the Apostle who had evangelised the Maltese during his three month stay on the island. The Maltese historians who defended the position of *Melita Africana* against that of *Melita Illyrica* were of great service to the cause of the Order of Saint John, and set out to do their task with enthusiasm. Let it suffice to state that Quintinus, whom we have quoted often in our study, stated that the whole island seemed to have been dedicated to Saint Paul.[112]

---

[112] Here I quote the English translation of the text of Quintinus, in VELLA (1980), 41-45: "The people are very devoted to their religion. Malta is consecrated to Saint Paul [*Divo Paulo consecrata est Melita*], and the people of this place once believed that he was God. Its religion is wonderfully practised in the whole island, both privately and publicly. A temple of very considerable proportions, to which is now attached the bishop's residence, is dedicated to Paul. Shrines are found all over the island. The people (guided as they claim by the annals of Luke) believe as firmly and with certainty that Paul has been in Malta just as much as they believe that Peter has been in Rome. They wish to make themselves appear to have derived this conviction by means of their skill in navigation, in which they are particularly experts. Where it is possible, I shall

The controversy did not live up to its expectations. Modern scientific biblical studies have all interpreted Luke's narrative as referring to Malta. The Mljet theory has been largely sidelined. Indeed, during the course of my visit to Dubrovnik, upon my remarks about Đurđević and his work and about the Mljet theory, I was surprised that few showed any particular inerest, since they regarded the whole question as being outdated. Nevertheless, as I have pointed out, there are still some Croatian historians who defend the theory, and some studies worthy of note have been published in these last decades. For me personally it has been interesting to come to know this enchanting island of Mljet and its ancient traditional link with the figure of Saint Paul.

Another pressing question, that has often been addressed without success, is that of pinpointing exactly the place where Paul was shipwrecked on Malta. Various theories have been proposed, some full of fantasy, others with a more scientific

---

now speak of this information as I have received it from them. I have thought it worth knowing, and it is just as pleasant to hear, especially for those who are fond of navigation. They therefore try to put the matter beyond dispute in this way. Paul (they say), leaving Crete from Clauda (according to Ptolemy it is *Claudus*, according to Pliny it is *Gaudos*, according to the present people it is *Gozo*) in mid-haven between the west and the south, and driven by those winds which Luke describes, could have been carried neither to Lesbus nor to Ionia, to which some divert Paul from Malta. If indeed he was carried by ship from Crete in that direction, he would have been carried not by the east winds, which were blowing diametrically opposite, but by the south winds. These winds left Paul at the time he was coasting round Crete, in that direction, when a whirlwind arose: the ship was caught in it and could not struggle against it any longer, nor could it hold its course to Italy. From Crete he was for sure driven by the east wind, which was then blowing, and he sailed towards Sicily in a full and untroubled sailing; and indeed the east wind would certainly have driven Paul from the island of Clauda straight on to Pachynus, a promontory of Sicily, had not (as the evangelist wrote) an εὐρακύλων arisen, or rather had not the east wind been accompanied with a swell and a tempest on the sea. In those days the sailors named that wind *Typhonicus* and, as Pliny says, it is the worst pest for navigation. Paul's ship, therefore, tossed about by this very violent and stormy east wind, having passed by Pachynus on the right and being very near Malta, which was then the nearest land to them, was caught by the force of the wind: and there the ship got stuck on a shore. From there (if this is at all worth telling) the journey is by sea to Rome, in the order given by Luke, through Syracuse, Reggio and Pozzuoli. Others take with a pinch of salt this north-easternly wind which one knows not what it is, and which (they say) is quite unknown to our sea and to our lands; and they wonder what new land in the whole world should be the one towards which, according to the interpreters of the account given in the Acts, this wind should have on that occasion blown. In this way the Maltese sailors include Paul in the history of their land: above all they point at and venerate his footsteps in many places. The shore of that place, which is between two seas, can actually be visited (according to Ptolemy it is called *Chersonesos*, as indeed it is); it has from very ancient times derived its name from Paul in as much as it is the site of the shipwreck. There is a small chapel in stone, not the least venerated in the island. Near the city there is a cave dug in a rock, with two altars within; they say that Paul was in custody in it for three months along with the other prisoners, healing at the same time the islanders who were vexed with various kinds of sickness and diseases, and calling them to Christ by his preaching."

basis. Everyone knows that, until solid archaeological proof in the seabed around Malta is found, which is quite difficult after two millennia, we will never know precisely where Paul was shipwrecked. The only valid theory is that upheld by popular tradition going back at the earliest to mediaeval times, indicating the area of Saint Paul's Bay as the place of the shipwreck. But which part of the bay? We will never know with absolute certainty. When I accompanied a group of Franciscan friars who work as Commissaries of the Holy Land to Saint Paul's Islet, during a congress organised in Malta, I proudly spoke about Selmunett as the "place between two seas" where Paul's ship had been shipwrecked. A professor of Scripture, Alfio Marcello Buscemi OFM, who was a speaker at the congress pulled me quietly aside and asked me: "This is a rocky islet. There is no sand here. How can you tell me that Paul was shipwrecked here when the Acts state that they wanted to run the ship aground on the beach?"

That same professor explained that Luke's aim in the Acts narrative is certainly not that of giving any specific geographical details, but simply that of stating how God's providence led him to Rome to announce the good news to the ends of the earth. His stop-over in Malta formed part of that providential plan. This is the true reason of the shipwreck of Saint Paul in *Melítē*. "I trust in God that things will turn out just as I was told; but we are to be stranded on some island" (Acts 27:25-26).

It is precisely this divine plan that brought Paul to *Melítē*. If this island was truly Malta, this means that Malta formed part of God's plan of salvation to be announced to all gentiles. This is the only logical conclusion of our analysis, even though all the rest is important and highly interesting. If this is so, then we still owe a debt of gratitude to the Apostle who gave us much more than he received from our generosity and kindness. Indeed, it is the same Apostle who continues to remind us, even after two millennia which have erased the original memories under the new modern and so-called progressive appearance of an island characterised by concrete forests of high-rise office blocks, hotels and congested roads: "It was I who fathered you in Christ Jesus, by the Gospel" (1Cor 4:15).

Index of Names and Places

View of the length of Mljet with the Veliko Jezero and Monastery of St. Mary

Islet of Sveta Marija, Mljet

National Park Mljet with the islet of Sveta Marija

Monastery of St. Mary, Mljet

View over Mljet National Park

Site of St. Paul's Shipwreck at Saplunara, Mljet

Roman ruins in Polače, Mljet

Odisejeva Špilja, Mljet

Remains of ancient Church near Korita, Mljet

Sveti Jakov Church, Dubrovnik

Satellite view of Crete. Gavdos islet lies on the SW of Cape Matala.
Mount Ida is in the centre of the island

Kaloi Limenes, Crete

Loutro, Crete

Psiloritis (Mount Ida), Crete

Gavdos

Cliffs of Gavdos

Satellite image of Malta. St Paul's Bay is visible on the NE coast between the Islet of Selmunett and Qawra Point

Aerial view of Selmunett

St. Paul's Islet

Munxar Point, Malta

ENE Gregale Gale at entrance to Grand Harbour, Malta

Għajn Rasul

San Pawl Milqi

St Paul's Grotto, Rabat

Fanum Iunonis. Archaeological remains at Tas-Silġ

View of St. Paul's Bay, Malta

Pietro Paolo Novelli, St. Paul healing Publius' father.
Chapel of St. Trophimus, Ta' Ġieżu Church, Valletta (1632)

Guido Reni (1575-1642), Saint Paul the Apostle